Biographies
to Read Aloud *with* Kids

Biographies
to Read Aloud with Kids

From Alvin Ailey *to* Zishe the Strongman

Rob Reid

an imprint of the American Library Association

HURON STREET PRESS

CHICAGO | 2014

Rob Reid is the author of read-aloud books for ALA Editions and Huron Street Press, including *Reid's Read-Alouds, Reid's Read-Alouds 2: Modern-Day Classics from C. S. Lewis to Lemony Snicket,* and *Silly Books to Read Aloud.* He has also written several books on children's and family story programming as well as books about children's music. Reid has a regular column in *Book Links* magazine, "Reid Aloud Alert," and also writes for *LibrarySparks* magazine. Reid is a senior lecturer in the Education Studies Department of the University of Wisconsin-Eau Claire, where he specializes in children's literature and literature for adolescents. He can be contacted via his website, www.rapnrob.com.

© 2014 by the American Library Association

Printed in the United States of America

18 17 16 15 14   5 4 3 2 1

Extensive effort has gone into ensuring the reliability of the information in this book; however, the publisher makes no warranty, express or implied, with respect to the material contained herein.

ISBN: 978-1-937589-57-8 (paper).

Library of Congress Control Number: 2013050277

Book design by Kim Thornton in the Charis SIL and Interstate typefaces.

♾ This paper meets the requirements of ANSI/NISO Z39.48–1992 (Permanence of Paper).

For David and Janna Morley

CONTENTS

ACKNOWLEDGMENTS

Thanks to:

Stef Zvirin, who suggested I write this book;

Book Links magazine for publishing my biography read-aloud article that Stef read;

The Cooperative Children's Book Center at the University of Wisconsin-Madison, the McIntyre Library at the University of Wisconsin-Eau Claire, and the Children's Literature Network as wonderful conduits of resources;

The Indianhead Federated Library System, the L. E. Phillips Memorial Public Library, and the Altoona (WI) Public Library for toting the large volume of requested books for this project;

University of Wisconsin-Eau Claire students Kirsten Marquette, Jozette Weber, and Jena Weiler for technical assistance;

Robert Burleigh, Kathleen Krull, and Jason Low for their insights on biographies for young people;

and all the children who listened and responded.

INTRODUCTION

As soon as I was old enough to learn how to read, back in the 1960s, I headed for the biography section of the library. I was particularly intrigued by presidents, inventors, and baseball players. Back then, some biographies for children were highly fictionalized and were fairly limited to the same figures we found in our school textbooks.

Many biographies written and illustrated for young people today are well documented with their factual research. The quality of writing is often lively and presents the facts in creative styles and formats. The children's publishing industry is a leader in showcasing a diverse choice of people to read about—many of them absent from our school's textbooks, but all playing important roles throughout history.

Readers are often inspired by the stories of real people, many who overcome hardships and barriers in their lives. Some of the lesser-known biographies are some of the most captivating. Robert Smalls, for example, was a slave who commandeered his owner's boat and slipped past several guard posts to freedom. Smalls went on to become a United States congressman. Maggie Gee was a Chinese American air force pilot during World War II, a time when not only was it rare for women to fly, but also at a time when Asian Americans were suspect of being spies for the enemy. Temple Grandin overcame merciless teasing about her autism and used her unique abilities to radically change the humane nature of the livestock industry. Chef

George Crum's impatience with a complaining customer inadvertently led to the invention of the potato chip. Biographies about well-known people often share little-known anecdotes about them, such as Dr. Seuss being voted "least likely to succeed" in college, or that George Washington was so unsure about his leadership abilities when given command of the American Continental Army that he had to read books on military strategies.

Categories and Styles of Biographies

This guide showcases two hundred biographies written for children ages four to fourteen. Some entries include an "also highly recommended" feature and point out additional biographies. Children's biographies today come in different categories and formats.

Picture book biographies have grown in popularity over the last several years and, in fact, constitute the majority of biographies in this guide. They can be read in one sitting. Most picture book biographies are between thirty-two and forty-eight pages in length and are aimed at an elementary and middle school level target audience, a slightly older readership than for fiction picture books that appeal mainly to preschoolers. Credit has been given to the illustrators in those citations since the pictures play an active role in telling the story. Let the children linger over the illustrations as you read picture book biographies; they'll pick up visual details that add to the story. Examples of picture book biographies in this guide are *The Librarian of Basra: A True Story from Iraq* by Jeanette Winter and *Martin de Porres: The Rose in the Desert* by Gary D. Schmidt.

Complete biographies cover the range of a person's entire life. Examples of complete biographies in this guide include *Amelia Lost: The Life and Disappearance of Amelia Earhart* by Candace Fleming and *Martha Graham: A Dancer's Life* by Russell Freedman. Partial biographies, on the other hand, highlight short aspects of a subject's life, such as Werner Franz's experience on the *Hindenburg* in *Surviving the* Hindenburg by Larry Verstrate and Bob Dylan's early musical career in *When Bob Met Woody* by Gary Golio.

Autobiographies, of course, are when people write about their own lives. Popular children's author Roald Dahl does so in *Boy: Tales of Childhood* as does Ji-li Jiang in *Red Scarf Girl: A Memoir of the Cultural Revolution.*

There are a couple of bilingual biographies listed in this book. Monica Brown wrote in both English and Spanish for her works *My Name Is Celia: The Life of Celia Cruz / Me llamo Celia: La vida de Celia Cruz* and *Pelé, King of Soccer / Pelé, el rey del fútbol.*

Graphic novel biographies have also increased in popularity. Despite their heavy dependence on the illustrations to tell the story, many graphic novels work well as read-alouds. While sharing them, be sure to read the dialogue balloons and sound effects in addition to the narration and let the kids linger over the pictures. Examples of graphic novel biographies are *Best Shot in the West: The Adventures of Nat Love* by Patricia C. McKissack, Frederick L. McKissack Jr., and Randy DuBurke and the autobiographical *Smile* by Raina Telgemeier.

The biographers use a variety of styles to tell the stories of their subject's lives. Many wrote poems and used the verse format, such as Marilyn Nelson's *Carver: A Life in Poems,* a biography of inventor George Washington Carver, and Patrick Lewis's book *Blackbeard, the Pirate King: Several Yarns Detailing the Legends, Myths, and Real-Life Adventures of History's Most Notorious Seaman.* Some biographers have their subjects describe their lives in a first-person delivery, such as S. D. Nelson's *Buffalo Bird Girl: A Hidatsa Story.* Other biographers chose unusual points of view. In her book *Play, Louis, Play! The True Story of a Boy and His Horn,* Muriel Harris Weinstein tells the real-life story of Louis Armstrong through the fictional device of his cornet speaking to the reader. In *The Adventures of Mark Twain by Huckleberry Finn,* Robert Burleigh tells us all about Mark Twain through the eyes of Twain's fictional creation, Huck Finn. These inventive style choices do not make these biographies works of fiction. Instead, they help make the real aspects of the subjects' lives interesting to listen to and read about.

While the majority of the biographies in this guide feature individuals and duos, collective biographies feature several people in one volume; these are highlighted in chapter 2. They often share something in common, such as the women in Catherine Thimmesh's *Girls Think of Everything: Stories of Ingenious Inventions by Women* and the females who trained for NASA's Mercury program in Tanya Lee Stone's *Almost Astronauts: 13 Women Who Dared to Dream.*

How the Biographies Were Chosen

Over the years, I've reviewed and shared over five hundred children's biographies with young people. For this guide, I narrowed the list down to two hundred exceptional biographies.

First, I looked for biographies written with a storyteller's flair. Again, that doesn't mean the storytelling aspects change the biographies into works of fiction. It means the biographers were creative in their approaches and styles to share someone's story. In the words of author Russell Freedman, biographies should "breathe life and meaning into people and events." Conscious of the fact that textbooks are dominated by stories of white males, I looked for a fairly even split between male and female subjects as well as representations of a diverse population.

Again, all selections were measured against the test: "is it a good story?" Biographies containing encyclopedic, dry writing styles, full of facts and short on anecdotes were not included. While I might purchase these formulaic biographies for a library collection for research purposes, I would not necessarily read them aloud to a young audience. I also did not include biographies of actors, athletes, musicians and other celebrities who are popular today but will most likely be forgotten in a few years. And I chose not to include biographies that had excessive strong language, difficult language and names to pronounce, or topics of personal matters, such as puberty. Those biographies are wonderful to read silently for individuals. Since the term "strong language" is subjective, I recommend readers scan each biography first before sharing it with children.

Finally, the biographies in this guide must appeal to children ages four through fourteen (preschool through middle school age). Kids are never too old to be read to. There is a misconception that adults should stop reading to young people when they learn to read themselves. Studies show that *listening* to stories makes one a better reader.

The Library as a Partner

Your local library will have access to most of the two hundred–plus biographies found in this guide. As I mention in my companion book *Silly Books to Read Aloud,* if your library doesn't own a copy of a particular book, they can access it from another library through interlibrary loan services. Most libraries have a "Suggestion for Purchase" service and might be able to buy a specific title for their collection.

Librarians also know where to find information about new biographies for children as they are published. Some of the resources they use, such as *Booklist* magazine, have a biography showcase issue each year. Let your librarian know you are interested, and she will keep an eye out for new, creative biographies as they appear on the market.

My read-aloud tips are simple: be yourself. You don't need to be overly theatrical in your delivery. The authors are skilled with words, often reading their own works out loud while writing or editing. If you follow their style, your delivery will be just right as you read to the children. I also recommend reading aloud any author notes, as well. They, too, add wonderful content and enrich the main story.

Finally, many children prefer nonfiction over fiction. Biographies are a wonderful way to feed this interest and help develop the love of reading. The two hundred titles in this guide are a great place to start. And with the pace the children's publishing industry is investing in producing well-written stories about creative and inspirational people, it won't be long before another two hundred high-quality biographies for young people are available on the market, meant to be read aloud. As Kathleen Krull states in her interview found in this book, "We're in the golden age of biographies for kids."

CHAPTER 1

Biographies of Individuals and Duos

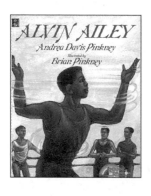

Alvin Ailey

Alvin Ailey. By Andrea Davis Pinkney. Illustrated by Brian Pinkney. Hyperion, 1993. 32 p. Ages 4–10.

Alvin was inspired by the hymns he heard at his Baptist church in Texas. These hymns would later have great influence on his work as one of America's greatest dancers and choreographers. Alvin and his mother moved to Los Angeles, where he was inspired by Katherine Dunham's modern dances. In 1949, Alvin had difficulty finding a dance studio that accepted black students. He finally learned that the Lester Horton Dance Theater School not only accepted students of all backgrounds, but taught the modern styles that fascinated Alvin. He soon created his own style; it came to him "the way daydreams do." Horton encouraged Alvin to draw upon his African American heritage for his choreography. Alvin moved to New York City and created the Alvin Ailey American Dance Theater. The biography ends with the triumph of Alvin's work *Revelations,* a piece full of gospel harmonies that "honored the heart and dignity of black people while showing that hope and joy are for everyone."

Louisa May Alcott
Louisa May's Battle: How the Civil War Led to Little Women. By Kathleen Krull. Illustrated by Carlyn Beccia. Walker, 2013. 48 p. Ages 8–12.

Louisa served as a volunteer nurse during the Civil War. The conditions in the makeshift hospital were horrible, but she worked hard to bolster the spirits of her patients. Louisa eventually became sick herself, succumbing to typhoid fever. She recuperated at her parents' home, spending two months in bed. She submitted some of her writing to publishers and got a particularly cruel rejection that read, "Stick to your teaching; you can't write." But Louisa knew she was a good writer. Her letters from the war hospital were published in a collection titled *Hospital Sketches*. She was then asked to write "a girls' book." She gathered her childhood memories, set the story during the Civil War, and wrote the memorable opening line, "Christmas won't be Christmas without any presents." That line, the book *Little Women,* and the author, Louisa May Alcott, became famous. Her greatest pride, however, was "that I had a very small share in the war which put an end to a great wrong."

Buzz Aldrin
Reaching for the Moon. By Buzz Aldrin. Illustrated by Wendell Minor. HarperCollins, 2005. 40 p. Ages 5–10.

Edwin Eugene Aldrin got his nickname from his two-year-old sister, who could not properly say the word *brother*. She pronounced it "Buzzer." "Later it got shortened to 'Buzz,' and no one ever called me anything else." Buzz felt destined to walk on the moon; his mother's maiden name was Moon. Buzz's father flew an airplane, and Buzz became fascinated with the notion of flying high at great speeds. He applied for the space program but knew that he needed to find a special skill that set him apart from everyone else. So Buzz studied aeronautics and astronautics and specialized in "rendezvous, learning how to bring two different objects together in space." Buzz wasn't accepted into the space program the first time, but he didn't give up. He flew up into space on *Gemini 12* and then on *Apollo 11*. Neil Armstrong was the first man to walk on the moon in 1969. Buzz was the second. Many people remember Armstrong's first words on the moon; Buzz's were, "Magnificent desolation."

Figure 1.1. From ***When Marian Sang: The True Recital of Marian Anderson*** by Pam Muñoz Ryan, illustrated by Brian Selznick.

Marian Anderson

When Marian Sang: The True Recital of Marian Anderson. By Pam Muñoz Ryan. Illustrated by Brian Selznick. Scholastic, 2002. 40 p. Ages 5–10.

Marian Anderson astonished folks with her remarkable singing. When she auditioned for master teacher Giuseppe Boghetti, he told her that he wasn't taking any new students. She quickly launched into a song, and Boghetti made room for her. Despite her fame, Marian wasn't allowed to sing at Constitution Hall in Washington, DC. Eleanor Roosevelt helped make arrangements for Marian to sing at the Lincoln Memorial. A crowd of seventy-five thousand cheering people showed up. Marian eventually realized her dream of performing at the Metropolitan Opera, the first African American to do so. Be sure to read the quote opposite the title page: "It was her range of notes that caused all the commotion. With one breath she sounded like rain, sprinkling high notes in the morning sun. And with the next she was thunder, resounding deep in a dark sky."

Also highly recommended: *The Voice That Challenged a Nation: Marian Anderson and the Struggle for Equal Rights.* By Russell Freedman. 114 p. Clarion, 2004. Ages 10–14. Freeman's biography of Anderson won a Newbery Honor Award and the Sibert Award for Best Informational Book of the Year.

Tillie Anderson

Tillie the Terrible Swede: How One Woman, a Sewing Needle, and a Bicycle Changed History. By Sue Stauffacher. Illustrated by Sarah McMenemy. Knopf, 2011. 40 p. Ages 4–10.

Tillie was working in a tailor's shop when she saw a man ride past on a bicycle. When Tillie finally got her own bike, she had trouble riding in dresses and skirts. She "used her noodle and her needle" and made a biking uniform that some folks found scandalous. Tillie entered her first bicycle race, one hundred miles long, and broke the woman's record by eighteen minutes. Her competitors often bumped her and punctured her tires. Tillie persisted and set another record during an eighteen-hour race in Chicago. She was called Tillie the Terrible Swede. Now complaints came from the male racers. They thought Tillie was too manlike. Doctors examined her and concluded that she was in better health because of the exercise. When they put a picture of her bare leg in the newspaper, folks were scandalized. Tillie was celebrated by women's right activist Susan B. Anthony, who said that "bicycling has done more to emancipate women than anything else in the world."

Roy Chapman Andrews

Dragon Bones and Dinosaur Eggs: A Photobiography of Explorer Roy Chapman Andrews. By Ann Bausum. National Geographic, 2000. 64 p. Ages 8–14.

Roy Chapman Andrews has been called the inspiration for the movie character Indiana Jones. This book mentions a number of Roy's narrow escapes, including being attacked by wild dogs, charged by an enraged whale, and falling off a cliff; Roy also joked, "I might have been killed by bandits." Roy led five expeditions to the Gobi Desert in Mongolia between 1922 and 1930. Like his movie counterpart Indiana Jones, Roy hated snakes. His crew named one worksite "Viper Camp" after a member of the expedition found snakes wrapped around each leg of his cot. The men were so jittery that Roy once leapt in fright from "a snake-size coil of rope." Roy's expeditions found the remains of a new kind of dinosaur named Protoceratops andrewsi, named in honor of Roy. They also discovered the remains of the first velociraptor and evidence that dinosaurs laid eggs. All in all, Roy and his crew "identified more than 380 new species of living and fossilized animals and plants."

Mary Anning

Stone Girl, Bone Girl: The Story of Mary Anning. By Laurence Anholt. Illustrated by Sheila Moxley. Orchard, 1998. 32p. Ages 4–9.

When she was a baby, Mary survived a lightning strike. Her father would take Mary to the cliffs near their home and show her treasures. Mary collected these treasures—fossils—and sold them to tourists despite being teased by other children, who cried, "Stone Girl, Bone Girl. Out-of-your-own-Girl!" A group of female scientists admired her fossils. They showed Mary a tooth from a large creature still hidden within the nearby cliffs. Mary finally found the remains of this "sea monster." It took six men to carry the bones, "as long as a tree and more than one hundred and sixty-five million years old." A museum bought this "fish lizard"—an ichthyosaur—and the money allowed Mary and her family to live comfortably the rest of their lives. The author's notes inform us that Mary was born in 1799 and lived in Lyme Regis in Dover, England. Mary went on to uncover other fossils and may have been the inspiration for the rhyme "She sells seashells by the seashore."

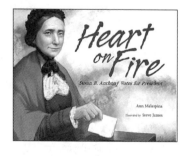

Susan B. Anthony

Heart on Fire: Susan B. Anthony Votes for President. By Ann Malaspina. Illustrated by Steve James. Albert Whitman, 2012. 32 p. Ages 6–10.

Four days before the 1872 presidential election, Susan B. Anthony ran to the voter registration office. Biographer Malaspina relates the events in free-verse format: "The inspectors looked up / shocked / and confused. / Only men could sign up to vote." Susan argued that the newly passed Fourteenth Amendment stated all persons born or naturalized in the United States are citizens of the country. The inspectors were stumped and allowed her to register to vote. Two weeks later, Susan was arrested and charged with voting. The law said she didn't have that right. Her lawyer paid her fine of one thousand dollars, but Susan still had to go to trial. The judge instructed the jury to find her guilty. Susan told the court, "You have trampled under foot / every vital principle of our government. / My natural rights, / my civil rights, / my political rights, / my judicial rights, / are all alike ignored." She was then told to pay an additional one hundred dollars. She never did, and Susan went on to speak out for equal rights for women the rest of her life.

Louis Armstrong

Play, Louis, Play! The True Story of a Boy and His Horn. By Muriel Harris Weinstein. Bloomsbury, 2010. 99 p. Ages 8–12.

Louis Armstrong's boyhood cornet narrates the musician's childhood story in this unusual point-of-view biography. Louis grew up in a rough neighborhood in New Orleans called the Battlefield. He was always interested in music and one day earned enough money to buy a used cornet from a "hock shop." One day, Louis took his mother's boyfriend's gun and fired it in the air. He was arrested and sent to the Colored Waif's Home for Boys. There, Louis found the discipline and structure he needed. He pitched in by doing hard work. He also learned a lot about music and, with the Colored Waif's Home Band, returned to his home neighborhood a hero. As Louis got older, he became an innovator of jazz music. When he played, his notes "turned colors: first blue, then purple, then spinning round like pink molasses and cotton candy, then into swirls of rainbow-colored ribbons." When he headed up to Chicago to make it big, Louis made sure to bring his childhood cornet along.

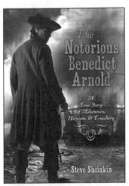

Benedict Arnold

The Notorious Benedict Arnold: A True Story of Adventure, Heroism, & Treachery. By Steve Sheinkin. Roaring Brook, 2010. 337 p. Ages 12–14.

Benedict Arnold's name is synonymous with the word *traitor*. Before he schemed for the British army, Benedict was actually a Revolutionary War hero. Even the British secretary of state wrote, "I think he has shown himself the most enterprising and dangerous man among the rebels." George Washington was impressed by Benedict on several occasions. At one point, he granted Benedict's request to invade Montreal through the Maine wilderness. Benedict led over one thousand men and three women up the Kennebec River. A summer drought made travel difficult. They were forced to portage thirteen miles over boggy conditions to another river: "The heavy boats scraped and rubbed the men's shoulders, wearing through their shirts, and then their skin, until the white tips of bones poked out." Benedict set up a plan to turn West Point over to the British. An amazing chain of events prevented this from happening. George Washington was dismayed to learn of Benedict's deceit: "Benedict Arnold, his courageous, unstoppable fighting general, the man he could always count on when others deserted him, had sold him out to the British."

Fred and Adele Astaire

Footwork: The Story of Fred and Adele Astaire.
By Roxane Orgill. Illustrated by Stéphane Jorisch.
Candlewick, 2007. 48 p. Ages 5–10.

Fred Astaire got his start as a dancer at the age of four when he put on ballet shoes at his sister Adele's dance class. "'Adele is a born dancer,' Father said, 'and Fred might not be too bad.'" In 1906, Fred and Adele became a vaudeville brother-sister act, dancing as a bride and groom on top of wooden wedding cakes. The two tap-danced, moved to the stage wings to watch the other acts, and then they "packed up their tubes of greasepaint, their wardrobe trunks, the two wedding cakes, and a few belongings and traveled to another theater in another town." When the siblings grew older, their big-time act was canceled. They were reduced to playing little theaters and once shared the bill with performing seals: "The Astaires had to climb a ladder to their dressing room, because the fishy-smelling seals got the only other dressing room, on the ground floor." Times were so poor that the two sometimes shared a hard-boiled egg for supper. The duo eventually made it to Broadway. When Adele married and stopped performing, Fred cast his eyes to Hollywood.

John James Audubon

Into the Woods: John James Audubon Lives His Dream. By Robert Burleigh.
Illustrated by Wendell Minor. Atheneum, 2003. 32p. Ages 5–10.

John James Audubon was a naturalist and painter best known for his drawings of birds. John always had a passion for studying animals and birds. Excerpts from John's journal are interspersed with biographer Burleigh's verse: "O

Father, dear Father, to me it seems / No one can fail who holds on to his dreams." He felt more at home in the forest than in town and wished he could draw it all. John captured a hawk in its nest and took it home. While the hawk clutched a stick of wood on John's desk, the artist made a pencil sketch. John opened a window once he was finished with the drawing: "I let it go and watched it fly, / A tiny speck against the sky." John realized time was passing "and I must paint it all because / We need this memory of what was."

Also highly recommended: *The Boy Who Drew Birds: A Story of John James Audubon.* By Jacqueline Davies. Illustrated by Melissa Sweet. Houghton Mifflin, 2004. 32 p. Ages 5–10. Young John watches birds from sunup to sundown and studies their habits.

Alia Muhammad Baker

The Librarian of Basra: A True Story from Iraq. By Jeanette Winter. Illustrated by the author. Harcourt, 2005. 32 p. Ages 4–10.

Alia Muhammad Baker was the city librarian of Basra, a port city in the country of Iraq. Alia worried as the talk of war began. She sought permission to move the books—many of them ancient—to a safer location. The governor refused, so Alia took matters into her own hands. She smuggled out books every night and put them in her car. Once the war began, Alia asked her friend Anis to help move the remaining books. He and others wrapped up the books in sacks and curtains. They passed them over a wall and into Anis's restaurant. Nine days later, the library burned to the ground. Alia hired a truck to move the thirty thousand rescued books from the restaurant to her own house and homes of friends. There were so many books in her house that she ran out of room for anything else. Alia dreamt that the war would end so they could build a new library. "But until then, the books are safe—safe with the librarian of Basra."

Josephine Baker

Jazz Age Josephine. By Jonah Winter. Illustrated by Marjorie Priceman. Atheneum, 2012. 40 p. Ages 4–10.

Singer-dancer Josephine Baker's story opens with a blues-style, lyrical verse and later switches to a jazz-style delivery. "People, listen to my story, 'bout a girl named Josephine. / People, listen to this story, 'bout a poor girl name of Josephine. / She was the saddest little sweetheart / this side of New Orleans." Josephine was born to a very poor family in St. Louis. As she grew up, she decided to act foolish for her friends and family, making faces and doing animal-style dance steps. People loved it. She left St. Louis after white folks

All through the night, Alia, Anis, his brothers, and shopkeepers and neighbors take the books from the library shelves, pass them over the seven-foot wall, and hide them in Anis's restaurant.

Figure 1.2. From *The Librarian of Basra: A True Story from Iraq* by Jeanette Winter, illustrated by the author.

burned down the black people's side of town. Josephine got her professional start as a chorus line dancer in New York City. She was forced to dress in blackface. Even though the white audiences loved it, Josephine knew that it was detrimental to her race. She left America for France, where she became a big star. It was 1925, and she finally felt free. She still longed for her home, where she was scorned for the color of her skin. But in Paris, she was able to turn her life into a jazzy fairy tale. "Zee-buh-dop zoo-buh-dop zee buh-dop ZOW! / Zop zop zop zop zoo-buh-dop ZOW!"

Clayton "Peg Leg" Bates

Knockin' on Wood: Starring Peg Leg Bates. By Lynne Barasch. Illustrated by the author. Lee & Low Books, 2004. 32 p. Ages 4–10.

Young Clayton loved to dance. He hated farming and would skip chores to dance at the town barbershop. When Clayton was twelve, he worked at a cottonseed mill. His leg got caught in the machinery and had to be amputated. "But it wasn't done in a hospital. No such thing was possible for a poor black boy in the south in 1919. The operation was performed at home by local doctors, on the kitchen table." Clayton made crutches out of old broomsticks. His uncle then made him a wooden leg—a peg leg. This enabled Clayton to dance again. He created his own style of tap dancing. Clayton became known as Peg Leg and performed for black audiences. He worked in bigger venues for white audiences and danced in blackface makeup to hide the fact that he was African American. He wasn't allowed to eat with the white performers. Finally, Peg Leg became so famous that he didn't need to wear a disguise. One of Peg Leg's quotes was "Don't look at me in sympathy, I'm glad that I'm this way. I feel good, knockin' on wood."

Ruth Becker

Escaping Titanic: A Young Girl's True Story of Survival. By Marybeth Lorbiecki. Illustrated by Kory S. Heinzen. Picture Window Books, 2012. 32 p. Ages 8–10.

Twelve-year-old Ruth Becker was a passenger on the *Titanic* with her mother and two siblings. One night, the engines stopped. A cabin steward told Ruth's mother that there had been a slight accident. A short time later, the passengers were instructed to head to the lifeboats. Ruth's mother shrieked when she noticed Ruth couldn't get in their boat: "Ruth, get into another boat!" Ruth was the last person allowed on that lifeboat. She watched in terror as the *Titanic* tilted. People jumped into the water. The ship split in half, its lights went out, and then the ship sank out of sight. Ruth felt helpless as she heard people wailing as they struggled in the ocean. "Then, slowly, a deathly quiet blanketed the water." Ruth's lifeboat was rescued by another ship, the *Carpathia.* The author's afterword mentions that Ruth was still alive when the remains of the *Titanic* were found in 1985. She died at the age of 90 in 1990, and her ashes were scattered over the sunken *Titanic.*

William Beebe

Into the Deep: The Life of Naturalist and Explorer William Beebe. By David Sheldon. Illustrated by the author. Charlesbridge, 2009. 48 p. Ages 5–10.

Will was fascinated by all aspects of wildlife. As a boy, he learned taxidermy, kept fish and snakes in his bedroom, and even raised a young owl named Moses. In 1928, Will's partner, Otis Barton, designed a deep-sea diving vessel. They called this two-and-a-half-ton creation a bathysphere. The two men tested it several times before going inside on their first exploration. During one of these tests, a small leak flooded the interior of the vessel and the force of the pressure shot the hatch like a bullet. In 1934, they finally descended into the deep ocean, where "Will was startled by an enormous creature gliding by them in the darkness." People today surmise that it was a giant squid. Will and Otis went down a half mile and found fish that emitted their own light. Will's "underwater journey opened up a new branch of scientific research into the deep seas." The author's notes state that Will's favorite research subjects were the hoatzin bird, the three-toed sloth, the ghost butterfly, the lantern fish, and the anglerfish.

Wilson Bentley

Snowflake Bentley. By Jacqueline Briggs Martin. Illustrated by Mary Azarian. Houghton Mifflin, 1998. 32p. Ages 4–10.

Willie Bentley loved winter. He compared the beauty of snow to butterflies and apple blossoms. Unfortunately, there was no way for anyone to share a snowflake with someone else. Snowflakes never repeat a design, and once they melt, "just that much beauty was gone, without leaving any record behind." Willie unsuccessfully tried drawing the different crystal patterns of the snowflakes. He got his first camera at the age of seventeen. It was a large camera, "taller than a newborn calf." Willie finally succeeded at capturing the image of a snowflake. Even though the neighbors scoffed, Willie knew the public would be interested in the photographs. The biography contains sidebars that can be read right along with the main narrative. One note tells us that a Valentine's Day snowstorm in 1928 lasted long enough for Willie to take over a hundred photographs: "He called the storm a gift from King Winter." Willie became known as the Snowflake Man. When he was sixty-six years old, a book of his photographs was published. Today, a monument in his hometown of Jericho, Vermont, honors the "world famous snowflake authority."

Blackbeard

Blackbeard, the Pirate King: Several Yarns Detailing the Legends, Myths, and Real-Life Adventures of History's Most Notorious Seaman. By J. Patrick Lewis. National Geographic, 2006. 32 p. Ages 8–12.

Edward Teach is famously known as Blackbeard. A dozen poems capture the excitement and suspense of his life. Short captions accompany most poems. The golden age of piracy was from 1698 to 1730, right after the Queen Anne's War left thousands of seamen jobless. Many of them turned to piracy. The first poem, "The Brethren of the Coast," informs us that none reached higher notoriety than Edward Teach. He named his ship *Queen Anne's Revenge.* "And who could say what horrified / Those hunted ships more / The specter of *Revenge* or / Its bearded commodore?" The poem "Edward Teach as Blackbeard" goes into detail about his striking appearance. He was tall and strong and had a "coal-black beard / Some said was the devil's mask." The two-part poem "The Battle of Ocracoke Inlet" gives details of Blackbeard's last battle. After boarding another ship, he was surrounded and killed. In true pirate fashion, the last poem, "At Teach's Hole," contains the haunting verse "The ghostly headless figure / Of Blackbeard, it is said / Still swims under the moonlight / Looking for its severed head."

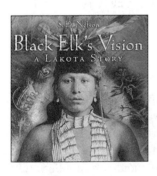

Black Elk

Black Elk's Vision: A Lakota Story. By S. D Nelson. Illustrated by the author. Abrams, 2010. 48 p. Ages 8–14.

When he was four years old, Black Elk had his first vision. A year later, he saw Cloud People, who told him, "Behold, a sacred voice is calling you." Black Elk didn't tell anybody about his vision. When he was nine, he became very sick. He had another vision and met the Six Grandfathers, who told him to respect the tree of life. A medicine man declared that Black Elk "had been blessed with a Great Vision." When he was twelve, Black Elk took part in the Battle of the Little Bighorn. Ten years later, he became part of Buffalo Bill's Wild West shows and traveled to New York City and Europe. After being shot at the Battle of Wounded Knee in 1890, Black Elk and his people were forced to move to Pine Ridge Reservation. Biographer Nelson tells this story through Black Elk's voice. As an old man, Black Elk tells the reader that he gives us the same gifts he received from the Six Grandfathers: "If you look with your heart, you will see the thirsty little tree before you. In your hands is the power to help it grow."

Elizabeth Blackwell

Who Says Women Can't Be Doctors? The Story of Elizabeth Blackwell. By Tanya Lee Stone. Illustrated by Marjorie Priceman. Holt, 2013. 40 p. Ages 5–10.

Back in the 1830s, Elizabeth was known to never walk away from a challenge. One of those tests came when a teacher "used a bull's eyeball to show students how eyes work." Even though she became queasy, Elizabeth developed coping techniques to help her stay strong. Elizabeth lived in a time when young women weren't allowed to be doctors. Many people laughed at her dream to become one. Twenty-eight medical schools turned down her applications. People said, "Women *cannot* be doctors. They *should not* be doctors." She was overjoyed when the Geneva Medical School in New York accepted her. However, few people actually wanted her there. The other students, all males, had voted to allow Elizabeth into the school, thinking it was all a joke. The joke backfired. Elizabeth worked hard and graduated with the highest honors. Elizabeth Blackwell had become the first female doctor in the United States. She still faced opposition—one male doctor wrote, "I hope, for the honor of humanity, that [she] will be the last." The biography ends with the line "But as you know, she certainly was NOT."

Amelia Bloomer

You Forgot Your Skirt, Amelia Bloomer! A Very Improper Story. By Shana Corey. Illustrated by Chelsey McLaren. Scholastic, 2000. 40 p. Ages 4–10.

In the eyes of many people, "Amelia Bloomer was NOT a proper lady." She fought for women to have the right to vote and started her own newspaper, called *The Lily.* Amelia thought that the clothing women were expected to wear was ridiculous. Dresses were very heavy. It was like "carting around a dozen bricks. They were so long that they swept up all the mud and trash from the street." Corsets were so tight, it was hard to breathe. Little girls were restricted in their movement and play. Amelia had a visit from her friend Elizabeth Cady Stanton and Elizabeth's cousin Libby. Libby wasn't wearing a dress. Her outfit "was NOT too heavy and NOT too long and NOT too tight and NOT too wide." Amelia made a similar outfit for herself that attracted a lot of attention. Many people were upset with these new outfits, called Bloomers. Amelia wrote an

Figure 1.3. From *You Forgot Your Skirt, Amelia Bloomer! A Very Improper Stor*y by Shana Corey, illustrated by Chelsey McLaren.

article about the new outfit in her newspaper, and "the circulation of THE LILY doubled almost overnight."

Nellie Bly

Bylines: A Photobiography of Nellie Bly. By Sue Macy. National Geographic, 2009. 64 p. Ages 10–14.

Elizabeth wrote a letter to a newspaper complaining about its viewpoints on the role of women. She was invited by the paper's editor to write her own article. She contributed a second article, this time under the pseudonym Nellie Bly, inspired by a popular Stephen Foster song. Nellie also wrote about the conditions of the Women's Lunatic Asylum on Blackwell Island in New York. She infiltrated the asylum by acting confused and tricking doctors into committing her. Her two-part account of abuse in the asylum led to massive improvements. Nellie was later inspired by Jules Verne's book *Around the World in Eighty Days*. She traveled around the globe and beat that title record by seven days. Nellie picked up a monkey on her trip and brought it to New York, "where he would make his presence felt in his new home by smashing all the dishes in her kitchen." When Nellie passed away in 1922, a newspaper tribute called her "THE BEST REPORTER IN AMERICA."

Louis Braille

Out of Darkness: The Story of Louis Braille. By Russell Freedman. Clarion, 1997. 81 p. Ages 8–12.

At the age of four, Louis Braille suffered a terrible accident when he stabbed himself in the eye with one of his father's sharp tools. The resulting infection spread to his other eye, and Louis became completely blind. A local priest made arrangements for him to attend the Royal Institute for Blind Youth in Paris. Meanwhile, Charles Barbier, a retired Army captain, developed a military code using raised dots and dashes. He brought this experiment to the school, but it was too hard for the students to master. Louis experimented with Barbier's system over the course of three years. Barbier's system was based on sounds; Louis developed one based on the letters of the alphabet. (Louis was fifteen years old when he finally made a breakthrough.) The students in the school welcomed this new method of reading. Unfortunately, the school director was replaced by a man who forbade the students from using Louis's system. After his initial reluctance, the new director relented. Louis died at the age of forty-two but is recognized for doing "more than anyone in history to bring blind people into the mainstream of life."

Laura Bridgman

She Touched the World: Laura Bridgman, Deaf-Blind Pioneer. By Sally Hobart Alexander and Robert Alexander. Clarion, 2008. 100 p. Ages 10–14.

In 1832, two-year-old Laura survived the scarlet fever that claimed the lives of two of her siblings. But the disease left Laura completely deaf and blind. She grew up on a New England farm and learned to identify everything by touch. Samuel Gridley Howe of the New England Institution for the Education of the Blind, the first American school for blind children, took an interest in Laura. He felt "her mind was a soul jailed to a body" and wanted to set her free. In the 1800s, many people believed the deaf and blind were impossible to educate. Laura blossomed at school, learning how to read and write. (She was frustrated with multiplication, however, and her teacher told her that she would understand it if she took the time to think about it. Laura responded by communicating, "My think is very tired.") Laura captured the public's imagination and became known to the country at the age of ten as an "educational masterpiece." Helen Keller's mother was inspired by Laura and realized that there was hope for her own daughter.

Barnum Brown

Barnum's Bones: How Barnum Brown Discovered the Most Famous Dinosaur in the World. By Tracey Fern. Illustrated by Boris Kulikov. Farrar, Straus and Giroux, 2012. 40 p. Ages 5–10.

Baby Barnum was so named in 1873 because his parents were fans of circus owner P. T. Barnum. Young Barnum grew up in Kansas, fascinated by the fossils unearthed by his father's plow. As a college student, he went on fossil hunts in South Dakota and Wyoming. Next Barnum got a job working for Henry Fairfield Osborn, administrator at the American Museum of Natural History in New York City. The museum didn't have a single dinosaur bone; it was Barnum's job to collect dinosaur and mammal fossils. He traveled all over the world, and he was good at his job—it was said that "he must be able to smell fossils." On one expedition in the Badlands, Barnum discovered bones unlike any he had ever seen before. He spent years trying to piece together the bone fragments. Osborn named the species Tyrannosaurus rex. "Barnum called it 'his favorite child.'" After more exploration, Barnum finally found "the treasure he had dreamed of—a perfect, four-foot-long *T. rex* skull."

Buffalo Bird Woman

Buffalo Bird Girl: A Hidatsa Story. By S. D. Nelson. Illustrated by the author. Abrams, 2013. 56 p. Ages 8–12.

Buffalo Bird Woman, a member of the Hidatsa people, was known as Buffalo Bird Girl when she was young: "This name has brought me fortune, for the buffalo have a strong heart and the birds of the air have a good spirit." Her role in the community was to cook, to farm, and to tan the hides of animals for clothing, shelter, and boats. Girls played with dolls and also participated in a game called hide-toss: "A group of girls held on to the edges of a large buffalo hide and used it to take turns tossing one another into the air." One summer day, Buffalo Bird Girl survived an attack from the Lakotas, who sought to enslave Hidatsa women and children. In her later years, Buffalo Bird Woman looked back on the life that was lost when the white government forced her people to give up their traditional ways and move to a reservation: "But I have not forgotten our old ways . . . In the shadows I seem again to see our Indian village, with smoke curling upward from the earth lodges."

Richard Byrd

Black Whiteness: Admiral Byrd Alone in the Antarctic. By Robert Burleigh. Illustrated by Walter Lyon Krudop. Atheneum, 1998. 40 p. Ages 8–12.

In 1934, Richard Byrd spent six months alone in Antarctica in a shack buried in the snow. He monitored eight weather instruments for scientists around the world. He also wanted to study how people lived in complete isolation. His journal entries are interspersed with biographer Burleigh's prose. When Richard turned on his lanterns in the tunnels, he wrote that the tunnels "take on a breathless radiance. Icicles on the roof glisten like candelabra." It was incredibly cold, even in the shelter. Richard was forced to keep the door open a little with the stove off to avoid deadly fumes. Unfortunately, one day carbon monoxide seeped into one of the tunnels. Richard felt at first that he was going to die. He then thought he heard "a very tiny voice: *Endure,* it says; *Live,* it says." A tractor team was sent to rescue Richard, but it was forced to head back twice due to dangerous weather conditions. Richard illuminated his location by dousing a kite tail with gasoline and lighting it on fire to create a beacon. The team found Richard and nursed him back to health.

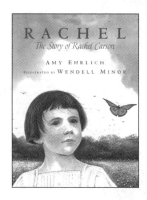

Rachel Carson

Rachel: The Story of Rachel Carson. By Amy Ehrlich. Illustrated by Wendell Minor. Harcourt, 2003. 32 p. Ages 5–10.

A young Rachel Carson found the fossil of a sea creature near her house in Pennsylvania. She was intrigued by the notion that her home at one time would have been under an ocean. In 1918, Rachel published a story titled "A Battle in the Clouds" in *St. Nicholas Magazine,* a periodical that showcased children's stories. In college, she studied biology. Rachel became a nature writer and specialized in articles about the ocean, helping her readers imagine life beneath the waves. In the 1950s, Rachel led a fight against people who sprayed poisons to kill mosquitoes. The poison also killed other insects as well as song-birds and fish. "The poisons were everywhere—on the grasses that cows ate, and in their milk and meat, and in our own bodies, too." Rachel's book *Silent Spring* warned of these dangers. The companies that made the poison attacked her work and said that "she was only a woman, after all, emotional and unreliable." The epilogue mentions that "today's environmental movement began with the publication of *Silent Spring.*"

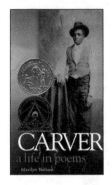

George Washington Carver

Carver: A Life in Poems. By Marilyn Nelson. Front Street, 2001. 103 p. Ages 11–14.

George Washington Carver was kidnapped as a baby in 1864. He was rescued and raised as a son by his white owners, Moses and Susan Carver. Biographer Nelson shares George's story in verse: "We whisper that our Green-Thumb Boy / is the black Mendel, that Darwin / would have made good use of Carver's eyes." George endured racial prejudice. One time, a new student from Arkansas raised a fuss—cleared his throat, rattled his tray, scraped his chair—when George sat at the same table for dinner. But George had the support of other students, who were white. When the Arkansas boy moved to their table, those students "cleared their throats, rattled their trays / and scraped their chair legs as they got up / and moved to Carver's table." George found a new home at the Tuskegee Institute. He inspired his students, sometimes taking them to the college dump where he rummaged around and held up an assortment of discarded objects. He asked them, "'Now, what can we do with this?' / Two by two, little lights go on. / One by hesitant one, dark hands are raised. / The waters of imagining, their element."

Ray Charles

Ray Charles. By Sharon Bell Mathis. Illustrated by George Ford. Lee & Low Books, 2001. 40 p. Ages 5–10.

Ray Charles developed a style of music that included elements of jazz and gos-pel. "His music has the power of a story. It tells about love and pain and joy and trouble. You can hear his tears in it." Ray lost his eyesight at an early age. His mother sent him to the St. Augustine School for the Blind, where Ray's fellow students once cruelly tricked him into running full speed into an iron post. Music helped Ray survive. He learned to read and write music through Braille:

"He would sit at the piano. His fingers would touch the first note pressed into the paper. Then he would touch the next note. He'd play these notes on the piano." Ray was soon making Braille arrangements for several instruments. He went on to become one of the most popular and honored musicians in the world. One high point in his life was when Ray refused to play to a segregated audience in Georgia. In appreciation of this gesture, he received "a collection of 8,500 signatures under the heading of one of his most famous songs, 'I Can't Stop Loving You.'"

Cesar Chavez

Harvesting Hope: The Story of Cesar Chavez. By Kathleen Krull. Illustrated by Yuyi Morales. Harcourt, 2003. 48 p. Ages 5–10.

When Cesar was a young boy, his family owned a prosperous ranch in Arizona. His mother taught her children an important lesson "against fighting, urging them to use their minds and mouths to work out conflicts." A drought left the family penniless, and they were forced to head to California to become migrant workers. The conditions were poor; they lived in a crowded old shed, and sometimes their meals consisted of dandelion greens. "Farm chores on someone else's farm instead of his own felt like a form of slavery." Cesar was humiliated at school for speaking his native Spanish. The teacher made him wear a sign that read, "I AM A CLOWN. I SPEAK SPANISH." As Cesar got older, he organized other workers to join him in a nonviolent strike. "*La Causa*—The Cause—was born." Cesar and others marched more than three hundred miles to the state capitol, leaving grapes to rot in the field. The wealthy landowners finally gave in and improved the workers' pay and working conditions.

Julia Child

Bon Appétit! The Delicious Life of Julia Child. By Jessie Hartland. Illustrated by the author. Schwartz & Wade Books, 2012. 48 p. Ages 6–10.

Julia Child was a tall gangly girl, with "VERY big feet." She loved to play pranks—she once painted a college dorm toilet seat with red paint. Julia got a job with the Office of Strategic Services during World War II. One of her tasks was to help develop a shark repellent to keep them away from underwater explosives. She fell in love with coworker Paul Child, and they discovered that they both liked exploring new foods and restaurants: "They have fish-head soup, ox tongue with tripe, snails, frogs, pig intestines, jellyfish with fish belly, pigs' ear with fish roe. Let's order it all! I'm hungry!" Julia was especially taken with French food. She worked for a very long time to help create a classic cookbook that became a best seller. This biography looks like a graphic novel with handwritten-style text that is not overly hard to read. There is a lot of humor scattered throughout. For instance, we see Julia's perspective while cooking on her television show; the cue card lady is holding up a sign that reads, "You have spinach in your teeth."

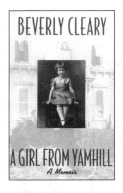

Beverly Cleary

A Girl from Yamhill: A Memoir. By Beverly Cleary. Morrow, 1988. 279 p. Ages 11–14.

Beverly grew up on a farm near Yamhill, Oregon. She recalls pouring a bottle of blue ink on the Thanksgiving tablecloth as a young child and "pat-a-pat, pat-a-pat, all around the table I go, inking handprints on that smooth white cloth." Another time, she climbed up onto the farmhouse roof. After her father retrieved her and asked what she was doing, Beverly replied that she was walking around the house. Her father responded with, "Next time do it on the ground." There were also hard times. When money ran short, the family moved to Portland. Beverly had been fearless on the farm but became anxious of her new surroundings. She gained confidence when she learned she won a writing contest, but she faltered again when informed she was the only one who entered. Finally, Beverly got the boost she needed when a teacher announced, "When Beverly grows up she should write children's books."

Also highly recommended: *My Own Two Feet: A Memoir.* By Beverly Cleary. 261 p. Morrow, 1995. Ages 12–14. Cleary continues telling her story from her college years to the publication of her first book *Henry Huggins.*

Roberto Clemente

Roberto Clemente: Pride of the Pittsburgh Pirates. By Jonah Winter. Illustrated by Raul Colón. Atheneum, 2005. 40 p. Ages 5–10.

Young Roberto grew up in Puerto Rico, where he had to make do with a guava tree branch for a baseball bat and a coffee-bean sack for a glove. Roberto was drafted by the Pittsburgh Pirates, a last-place team. The announcer didn't know how to pronounce Roberto's name during his first time at bat: "ROB, uh, ROE . . . BURRT, um, let's see, TOE CLUH-MAINT?" Roberto introduced *himself* with a base hit. Kids imitated the cool way he twisted his neck as he came to bat. He helped lead the Pirates to the World Series. Despite Roberto's accomplishments, sportswriters were very critical of him. They mocked his Spanish accent and called him lazy and hotheaded. "'It's because I'm black, isn't it?' he asked the sneering reporters." Roberto was proud of his Puerto Rican heritage. After his many accomplishments on the field, Roberto lost his life trying to help earthquake victims in Central America when the plane he was on fell into the ocean. "When someone like Roberto dies, his spirit lives on in the hearts of all he touched."

Alice Coachman
Touch the Sky: Alice Coachman, Olympic High Jumper. By Ann Malaspina. Illustrated by Eric Velasquez. Albert Whitman, 2012. 32 p. Ages 5–10.

Alice loved to run and play basketball with the boys. Her father scolded her for not acting like a lady. One of her teachers took her to a track meet, where she became fascinated with the high jump. Alice and her friends constructed one out of sticks and rags. Alice's trademark was to suck on a lemon before her jumps. Biographer Malaspina uses verse format to share Alice's life: "The lemon made her feel / lightning-fast / feather-light, moon-jumping strong." She won first place and was invited to join the famous Tuskegee Golden Tigerettes. She went on to win her first national medal. Alice's dreams of winning an Olympic medal were crushed when the games were canceled because of World War II. Alice wondered if her time had passed by. But she competed in the 1948 Olympic Trials and set a record. At the London Olympic Games, Alice won the gold medal and set a new Olympic record. She was also the first African American woman to win an Olympic gold medal. "Alice had finally touched the sky."

Elizabeth Coleman
Talkin' about Bessie: The Story of Aviator Elizabeth Coleman. By Nikki Grimes. Illustrated by E. B. Lewis. Orchard, 2002. 48 p. Ages 5–10.

Several narrators share their memories of barnstorming pilot Elizabeth Coleman. Her father recalls her birth in a dirt-floor cabin on a cold winter day in 1892. A schoolteacher remembers how Bessie hoarded knowledge like a miser with gold coins. A white customer noticed that Bessie would look her in the eyes, something unusual for a black child: "You know, like we were *equals*." Bessie made up her mind to become the first black woman to fly. She moved to Paris and witnessed a crash at the school. A flight instructor said, "I was surprised the next day when she came for her lesson, how she boarded the plane without hesitation." Bessie returned to America, and even though her first flying exhibition had a small turnout, one reporter recognized the wonder of the moment: "I knew how far Bessie had brought us all. None that mild September day applauded more loudly, or proudly, than I."

Claudette Colvin

Claudette Colvin: Twice toward Justice. By Phillip Hoose. Melanie Kroupra, 2009. 133 p. Ages 12–14.

Nine months before Rosa Parks made her famous stand on a Montgomery, Alabama, bus, a teenage girl refused to give up her bus seat to a white woman in the same city. That day, Claudette boarded a city bus with her classmates after school. The bus started filling up, and Claudette was ordered by the bus driver to give up her seat. "Rebellion was on my mind that day. All during February we'd been talking about people who had taken stands." The bus driver pulled over to let two white policemen board the bus. (The language the police used with Claudette is strong, so be aware when reading that particular passage.) Claudette Colvin was arrested, taken to jail, and later found guilty of violating segregation laws, disturbing the peace, and resisting arrest. Her parents and Pastor Reverend Johnson bailed her out. Afterward Johnson told Claudette, "I think you just brought the revolution to Montgomery." Unfortunately, Claudette has been largely forgotten in history as one of the first to challenge Jim Crow laws in Montgomery.

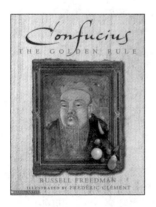

Confucius

Confucius: The Golden Rule. By Russell Freedman. Illustrated by Frédéric Clément. Scholastic, 2002. 48 p. Ages 10–14.

Confucius was born as Kong Qiu (kong chyoh) around 551 BC in what is now known as Shandong Province in China. Confucius studied intensively but was also a strong man skilled with the bow and arrow and the handling of horses. "He has been described as a homely giant with warts on his nose, two long front teeth that protruded over his lower lip, and a wispy beard." Even though he was a lowly government official, Confucius was very persuasive and developed a large following of students. They wanted to bring reforms to China, including those concerning education: "When people are educated, distinction between classes disappear." Confucius took several students on dangerous journeys. At one point, he was mistaken for a bandit and thrown into prison. Still, it was noted that he felt at ease at most places he visited: "I listen carefully, pick out what is best, and follow it myself. I see many things and remember them." The endpapers are decorated with sayings from *The Analects of Confucius,* such as "I am fortunate indeed. Whenever I make a mistake, there is always someone to notice it."

Jacques Cousteau

Manfish: A Story of Jacques Cousteau. By Jennifer Berne. Illustrated by Eric Puybaret. Chronicle, 2008. 32 p. Ages 5–10.

Jacques loved all aspects of water. When a friend gave Jacques goggles, a whole new magical underwater world opened up for him. He created an underwater camera to record his diving journeys. Jacques wanted to breathe underwater for a long time, to become a "manfish." He realized that dream with the newly invented aqualung: "Now he could swim across miles of ocean, his body feeling what only scales had felt, his eyes seeing what only fish had seen." He turned an old warship named the *Calypso* into a scientific explorer ship. Jacques and his crew filmed the underwater world and aired these movies in theaters and on television. They attracted large audiences who were viewing underwater images for the very first time. Jacques discovered that many parts of the ocean were polluted by garbage and toxic chemicals. His movies warned people, including world leaders. "And he spoke to children. Jacques dreamed that someday it would be you, exploring worlds never seen, never imagined . . . Worlds that are now yours."

George Crum

George Crum and the Saratoga Chip. By Gaylia Taylor. Illustrated by Frank Morrison. Lee & Low Books, 2006. 32 p. Ages 5–10.

George and his sister Kate were treated poorly because they were part Native American and part African American. George didn't let that stop him from becoming an innovative chef. He met a Frenchman who taught him how to cook over open flame. George landed a job at one of the best restaurants in Saratoga Springs, New York. He became a popular chef but often lost his temper with fussy customers. One day in 1853, a woman complained her French-fried potatoes were cut too thick. George was upset and decided to teach that person a lesson. He cut the potatoes extremely thin and cooked them in hot oil longer and at a higher temperature than usual. The woman "declared them the most delicious potato delicacy she had ever tasted!" George was stunned. His Saratoga Chips became a big hit, and the potato chip was invented. George went on to open his own popular restaurant where customers, no matter how rich or poor they were, "light-skinned or dark, young or old, female or male . . . had to wait just the same, because everyone was equal at Crum's Place!"

Celia Cruz

My Name Is Celia: The Life of Celia Cruz / Me llamo Celia: La vida de Celia Cruz. By Monica Brown. Illustrated by Rafael López. Rising Moon, 2002. 32 p. Ages 5–10.

Celia was the Queen of Salsa. Her singing made everyone feel like dancing. The bilingual text captures the lively feel to Celia's music: "Boom boom boom! beat the congas. Clap clap clap! go the hands. Shake shake shake! go the hips. . . . *¡Bum bum bum! resuenan las tumbadoras. Las manos aplaudén y las caderas se menean.*" Celia grew up in Havana, Cuba. She helped her mother put the younger children to sleep by singing lullabies. Celia was encouraged by a teacher to sing. "Your voice is a gift from above and must ring sweet in the ears of our people." She entered singing competitions but was sometimes not allowed to compete because of the color of her skin. Celia made a new home in America and became famous.

Also highly recommended: *Tito Puente, Mambo King / Tito Puente, Rey del Mambo.* By Monica Brown. Illustrated by Rafael López. HarperCollins, 2013. 32 p. Ages 5–10. Musician Tito Puente's biography is set up in a very similar bilingual text with a lively music cadence to the words.

Marie Curie

Something Out of Nothing: Marie Curie and Radium. By Carla Killough McClafferty. Farrar, Straus and Giroux, 2006. 134 p. Ages 10–14.

Poland was occupied by Russia in 1877. A Russian inspector entered young Manya's classroom to test the Polish students on their knowledge and loyalty to Russia: "'Who rules over us?' he demanded." Manya was the one chosen to acknowledge that "the tsar" was the correct answer. Manya grew up to become Marie when she registered for college at the Sorbonne in Paris. She became the first woman to earn a master's degree in physics at that institution. Marie went on to achieve many other "firsts," including becoming the first woman to earn a doctorate in France, the first woman to win a Nobel Prize, and the first person to win two Nobel Prizes. Marie discovered two new elements: polonium, named after her home country Poland, and radium. She and her husband, Pierre, suffered healthwise due to their exposure of radium. Surprisingly, many companies used radium in everyday products before stricter laws regulated its use. These included toothpaste, bathing powder, soap, and fishing lures. Years after Marie's death, the French government moved her remains, along with her husband's, "to the Pantheon, where some of France's most famous dead are laid to rest." She "was the first woman to be given this honor on her own merit."

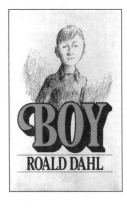

Roald Dahl

Boy: Tales of Childhood. By Roald Dahl. Farrar, Straus and Giroux, 1984. 160 p. Ages 9–14.

Some of this children's author's childhood memories "are funny. Some are painful. Some are unpleasant . . . All are true." Roald and his friends frequented a sweet-shop. It was owned by Mrs. Pritchett, a nasty woman who stuck her filthy hands in the candy jars and yelled at the boys. Roald came up with the brilliant idea to place a dead mouse in one of the jars. The next day, the shop was closed. The boys worried that they had killed the owner from shock. Instead, Mrs. Pratchett showed up at school, identified the boys, and watched as the headmaster caned them on their bottoms. She exited the school saying, "Right in the jar of Gobstoppers it was! A stinkin' dead mouse which I will never forget as long as I live!" Another time, Roald filled his sister's boyfriend's pipe with goat droppings while the rest of the family watched in conspiratorial silence.

Also highly recommended: *Going Solo.* By Roald Dahl. Farrar, Straus and Giroux, 1986. 208 p. Ages 12–14. Roald continues his story as a young man flying a fighter plane in World War II.

Charles Darwin

Charles Darwin. By Alice B. McGinty. Illustrated by Mary Azarian. Houghton, 2009. 48 p. Ages 5–10.

Biographer McGinty combines her story with entries from Charles Darwin's journal. Charles and his brother concocted smelly chemistry experiments that earned him the nickname "Gas." When Charles had an opportunity to travel on the *HMS Beagle,* he was almost rejected by the ship's captain, who didn't like the shape of Charles's nose. Charles developed theories of change in the natural world that went against his religious beliefs. In 1859, Charles published his controversial work *The Origin of the Species.* One of his friend's reacted by saying, "I have read your book with more pain than pleasure." Over the years, however, his book sold millions of copies. Charles's next book, *The Descent of*

Man, discussed his thoughts on evolution. People today still argue over his theories. The biography ends with this journal entry: "I have worked as hard and as well as I could, and no man can do more than that."

Also highly recommended: *Charles and Emma: The Darwins' Leap of Faith.* By Deborah Heiligman. Henry Holt, 2009. 320 p. Ages 12–14. Charles and Emma's courtship and marriage are covered, as well as their religious struggles with Charles's controversial theories.

John Bul Dau and Martha Arual Akech

Lost Boy, Lost Girl: Escaping Civil War in Sudan. By John Bul Dau and Martha Arual Akech. National Geographic, 2010. 159 p. Ages 12–14.

John, a country boy from Southern Sudan, and Martha, a city girl from Juba, both became separated from their families and were forced to flee from armies during the Sudan Civil War of 1983–2005. Alternating chapters capture their first-person narratives as they walked hundreds of miles to Ethiopia and then Kenya. John's village was attacked when he was thirteen years old. His long walk to freedom was constantly threatened by soldiers. In one of Martha's passages, she and her sister made it to a refugee camp in Ethiopia. While life was hard, Martha made friends and went to church. After three years at the camp, Martha was forced to leave because of encroaching violence. John and Martha eventually met and became a couple: "Since John was a Lost Boy and I was a Lost Girl, we had a lot of background in common." After the two married and moved to America, Martha declared, "I'm not lost anymore."

Tomie dePaola

26 Fairmount Avenue. By Tomie dePaola. Putnam, 1999. 58 p. Ages 4–9.

Tomie visited his great-grandmother Nana Upstairs one day. While rummaging around, he found chocolates in the medicine cabinet and shared the whole packet with her. The chocolates were actually laxatives. Tomie states, "Both Nana Upstairs and I didn't feel so good, and I think we both made a mess." Tomie was allowed to draw pictures on the walls of his new home while it was under construction. When the plasterers covered up Tomie's drawings, his grandfather Tom made him feel better by saying that the pictures would always be there, preserved. Kindergartener Tomie was upset that he wouldn't be taught how to read until first grade. He turned around that first day of school and headed back home. His mother convinced him that he needed to pass kindergarten or he'd never learn to read. "So I went back to school, but I never really liked kindergarten."

Also highly recommended: *Here We All Are.* By Tomie dePaola. Putnam, 2000. 67 p. The popular children's author/illustrator shares more of his childhood in this second volume of the 26 Fairmount Avenue series. The other titles are *On My Way* (2001), *What a Year!* (2002), *Things Will Never Be the Same* (2003), *I'm Still Scared* (2006), *Why? The War Years* (2007), and *For the Duration* (2009).

Dave Drake
Etched in Clay: The Life of Dave, Enslaved Potter and Poet. By Andrea Cheng. Lee & Low Books, 2012. 143 p. Ages 10–14.

In the early 1800s, a South Carolina pottery manufacturer purchased a young slave and named him Dave. Dave's job was to haul heavy clay from the river banks. His master noticed Dave's interest in making pottery and let him work the clay, although the master worried that Dave would forget his place. Dave endured much hardship in his life. He was sold to different owners and lost two wives and two stepsons. He also lost a leg in a train accident. There was danger, too, for Dave had learned to read and write. Biographer Cheng tells Dave's story in verse: "A slave who can read / is one thing, / but a slave who can write / is a menace." Dave started etching poems into the pottery. "Be careful, Dave. / Those words in clay / can get you killed." Dave continued to defy the system and his owners: "But when I write / I am a man."

Also highly recommended: *Dave the Potter: Artist, Poet, Slave.* By Laban Carrick Hill. Illustrated by Bryan Collier. Little, Brown, 2010. 40 p. Ages 5–9. This picture book version of Dave's story earned the Coretta Scott King Award and Caldecott Honor Award for illustrator Collier.

Bob Dylan
When Bob Met Woody: The Story of the Young Bob Dylan. By Gary Golio. Illustrated by Marc Burckhardt. Little, Brown, 2011. 40 p. Ages 8–12.

Robert Zimmerman "floated into this world on waves of sound." Bob grew up in the northern Minnesota mining town of Hibbing, where he taught himself piano and guitar. During a high school talent show, Bob and his band got kicked off the stage for being too loud. He was influenced by the writing of John Steinbeck and the poetry of Dylan Thomas. Bob even changed his last name to Dylan in honor of his favorite poet. After high school, Bob found the

Figure 1.4. From ***When Bob Met Woody: The Story of the Young Bob Dylan*** by Gary Golio, illustrated by Marc Burckhardt.

music of Woody Guthrie, a folksinger known mostly for his song "This Land Is Your Land": "Woody's words were like a compass, pointing the way to a bigger, brighter world." In 1961, Bob learned that Woody was hospitalized near New York City and set out hitchhiking. The two met, and Bob sang Woody's songs back to him. Bob was later invited to see Woody again at a friend's house. Bob pulled out his guitar and played the first real folk song he wrote, "A Song for Woody." "When Bob finished, Woody's face lit up like the sun."

Amelia Earhart

Amelia Lost: The Life and Disappearance of Amelia Earhart. By Candace Fleming. Schwartz & Wade Books, 2011. 118 p. Ages 10–14.

Amelia was an adventurous girl who said "the rules of female conduct bewildered and annoyed me." When she was older, Amelia watched a stunt plane exhibition and believed "that little red airplane said something to me as it swished by." Amelia became an overnight celebrity when she was the first female to fly in a plane across the Atlantic Ocean. While she stated she didn't crave publicity, her sister noted that she "never objected to it." In 1932, Amelia became the first woman to fly solo across the Atlantic. Amelia next wanted to fly around the globe. After Amelia was lost at sea and declared dead, her husband, George, worried about her legacy. (There were many unfounded rumors spurred on by the public's imagination. For example, some people thought she had been rescued by a Japanese fishing boat but was now that country's prisoner.) Biographer Fleming writes that Amelia encouraged women "to challenge themselves and seize their dreams. And she did it with zest, boldness and courage."

Also highly recommended: *Night Flight: Amelia Earhart Crosses the Atlantic.* By Robert Burleigh. Illustrated by Wendell Minor. Simon & Schuster, 2011. 36 p. Ages 4–10. When Amelia became the first woman to fly solo over the Atlantic, she "knows she crossed more than an ocean."

Sylvia Earle
Life in the Ocean: The Story of Oceanographer Sylvia Earle. By Claire A. Nivola. Farrar, Straus and Giroux, 2012. 32 p. Ages 5–10.

Sylvia Earle spent more than seven thousand hours underwater in the ocean, what she called "the blue heart of the planet." As a young girl, she spent hours observing nature, first on her parents' farm in New Jersey and then at their new home in Florida. As Sylvia grew up, she was the only woman on a research ship in the Indian Ocean. Other accomplishments included leading a team of divers to a deep-sea laboratory, descending three thousand feet in the Pacific Ocean in a one-person bubble she helped design, and swimming alongside whales. Sylvia learned that daytime fish tucked into the same "nooks and crevices" the nighttime fish vacated, and that they all returned to those same homes. She once traveled 1,250 feet deep in the waters off Hawaii, "deeper than anyone has ever walked!" Sylvia was fascinated by the bioluminescent creatures and felt that she was "diving into a galaxy." She became a spokeswoman "for the vital importance of the ocean to the health of our planet and to our very survival."

Gertrude Ederle
America's Champion Swimmer: Gertrude Ederle. By David A. Adler. Illustrated by Terry Widener. Harcourt, 2000. 32 p. Ages 5–10.

When Trudy Ederle was a young girl, she nearly drowned in a pond. Her father turned Trudy into a strong swimmer by tying a rope around her waist, holding the other end, and making her dog paddle as hard as she could. Trudy went on to set twenty-seven U.S. and world records as well as three medals at the 1924

Olympics. She next took on the challenge of swimming the English Channel. No woman had ever done so before, and only five men had accomplished this feat. She failed in her first attempt after fighting the strong current for nine hours. A year later, she tried again. The support crew's tugboat had an arrow pointing to England on the side with the words "THIS WAY, OLE KID" written in chalk. Trudy "ate chicken and drank beef broth" while floating during short breaks. That afternoon, a storm arrived and Trudy's crew told her to quit. Trudy kept swimming and arrived in England with thousands of spectators waiting on shore. She had beaten the men's record by almost two hours. "'I knew if it could be done, it had to be done, and I did it,' Trudy said after she got ashore. 'All women of the world will celebrate.'"

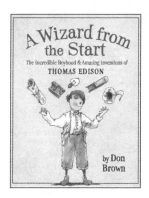

Thomas Edison

A Wizard from the Start: The Incredible Boyhood & Amazing Inventions of Thomas Edison. By Don Brown. Illustrated by the author. Houghton Mifflin, 2010. 32 p. Ages 5–10.

Tom's teacher called him "addled . . . another way of calling Tom confused or stupid." So his mother yanked him out of school and taught him herself. Tom read many books and was inspired to make his own chemistry set in the cellar; his mother worried that Tom and his friend "would blow [their] heads off." When he was twelve, Tom worked aboard trains selling newspapers, cigars, and snacks to the passengers. He accidentally started a fire on the train and got his ears boxed by an angry railroad worker. This may have been the cause of Tom's hearing loss. Tom also saved the life of a telegraph operator's child, and the father gave Tom telegraph lessons. At the age of twenty-two, Tom invented an electric vote-recording machine. It was his first patent. No one wanted the machine, but Tom kept tinkering. He invented the electric lightbulb in 1879. He went on to earn 1,093 patents in his life. Some of Tom's inventions include an electric storage battery, the phonograph, and the motion picture camera. Tom often said, "I never did a day's work in my life. It was all fun."

Sarah Edmonds

Nurse, Soldier, Spy: The Story of Sarah Edmonds, a Civil War Hero. By Marissa Moss. Illustrated by John Hendrix. Abrams, 2011. 48 p. Ages 5–10.

Nineteen-year-old Sarah Edmonds dressed as a man to escape an arranged marriage. She left her home in Canada and crossed the border into the United

States. Sarah signed up as a soldier but was turned away; not for being a female—she was disguised—but for being too young. On her second attempt to enlist, she succeeded. Sarah fought in several battles, including Bull Run and the Battle of Fair Oaks. She served for a while as a nurse, "something only men with the strongest stomachs did because of the long, draining hours and horrors of surgery without anesthetic." Sarah was then enlisted as a spy. When asked to help out in this role, Sarah's reply was "I'M YOUR MAN!" She was sent to the Confederate camp and learned valuable information, such as the number of cannons the Confederates had, as well as the number of "logs that had been painted black and set up to look like cannons from a distance." When she returned from her mission successfully, she realized freedom wasn't to be taken for granted: "It was something to fight for, to cherish."

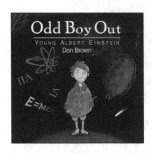

Albert Einstein

Odd Boy Out: Young Albert Einstein. By Don Brown. Illustrated by the author. Houghton Mifflin, 2004. 32 p. Ages 5–10.

Albert was a quiet child growing up. When he did speak, his words were often "clever and sharp." Albert also had a nasty temper, sometimes throwing tantrums: "His temper so terrifies a tutor hired to help young Albert prepare for school that she runs away, never to be seen again." Albert did devote a lot of attention and concentration to the things he enjoyed, such as learning the working of a compass and building a stack of playing cards fourteen stories high. At school, Albert was often the target of bullies, who made fun of him for being Jewish. One teacher told Albert that "he would never get anywhere in life." Eventually, Albert grew up to show the world ideas of "space and time and energy and matter that no one has ever seen before." The biography concludes with the line "For the world, *Einstein* comes to mean not fat baby, or angry child, or odd boy, but great thinker."

Also highly recommended: *Albert Einstein.* By Kathleen Krull. Viking, 2009. 141 p. Ages 10–14. Biographer Krull's account will hook readers with the opening line, "Albert Einstein had major bedhead."

Duke Ellington

Duke Ellington: The Piano Prince and His Orchestra. By Andrea Davis Pinkney. Illustrated by Brian Pinkney. Hyperion, 1998. 32 p. Ages 5–10.

Young Edward Kennedy Ellington told everyone to call him Duke. "He was a smooth-talkin,' slick-steppin,' piano-playin' kid." He was disgusted with his

The ragtime music set Duke's fingers to wiggling. Soon he was back at the piano, trying to plunk out his own ragtime rhythm. *One-and-two-and-one-and-two* . . . At first, this was the only crude tinkling Duke knew.

Figure 1.5. From ***Duke Ellington: The Piano Prince and His Orchestra***
by Andrea Davis Pinkney, illustrated by Brian Pinkney.

piano lessons as a young boy and quit. Years later, he heard ragtime music and was inspired to play once more. Duke developed his own style. He put together a band, and they became regulars at the Cotton Club in Harlem. Duke became even more popular when his music was broadcast live over the radio. Some of his most famous titles included "Creole Love Call," "Mood Indigo," and "Take the 'A' Train." Duke encouraged his band members to improvise their solos: "Yeah, those solos were kickin.' Hot buttered bop, with lots of sassy-cool tones." Duke celebrated the history of African American people with his composition "Black, Brown, and Beige." Duke Ellington and His Orchestra premiered the suite at Carnegie Hall in 1943, a place few African Americans had played before. We learn in the author's notes that Duke Ellington wrote and composed over one thousand compositions in his life.

Eratosthenes
The Librarian Who Measured the Earth. By Kathryn Lasky. Illustrated by Kevin Hawkes. Little, Brown, 1994. 48 p. Ages 5–10.

A Greek boy named Eratosthenes (AIR-uh-TOS-thun-neez) served as a tutor to the sons of the king of Egypt. The city of Alexandria was an exciting place, with the best library and museum in the world. Eventually, Eratosthenes became the head librarian. He helped scholars find information and worked on his own research as well. Geography was his main interest. He wanted to measure how big around the earth was. He pieced together his research from different scrolls in the library and set out to write the first geography book. The book wouldn't be complete, however, without knowing the circumference of the earth. Eratosthenes developed a system that required the king's best "bematists—surveyors trained to walk with equal steps," since camels were too stubborn and ornery to be accurate. In the end, "Eratosthenes' measurements provided the first accurate, mathematically based map of the world." Indeed, his ancient calculations were proven with modern-day measurements to be off by only a two-hundred-mile difference.

Philo Farnsworth
The Boy Who Invented TV: The Story of Philo Farnsworth. By Kathleen Krull. Illustrated by Greg Couch. Knopf, 2009. 40 p. Ages 7–12.

Philo was a thinker who was in awe of Alexander Graham Bell, the inventor of the telephone, and Thomas Edison, the inventor of the phonograph. Scientists knew about the concept of television before it was invented. However, they were stumped on how to send pictures through the air. After gazing at the parallel rows of potatoes in a field, Philo "saw a way to create television: breaking down images into parallel lines of light, capturing them and transmitting them as electrons, then reassembling them on a viewer." It still took a long time for Philo to be able to make one. He was obsessed and even told his new wife, "There is another woman in my life—and her name is Television." At the age of twenty-two, Philo was finally able to show a blurry image of a straight line, and later a dollar sign, and cigarette smoke. "He was a real inventor, likes his heroes—someone who connected people, a shaper of the world to come. Thanks to him, the future would include TV."

Ella Fitzgerald

Skit-Scat Raggedy Cat: Ella Fitzgerald. By Roxane Orgill. Illustrated by Sean Qualls. Candlewick, 2010. 48 p. Ages 5–10.

There was music in young Ella's house in 1930: "I'm a rowdy dowdy that's me / She's a high hat baby that's she . . ." Ella saved her nickels to ride the trolley to Harlem, "forty-five minutes and a world away." She learned and danced the Lindy Hop and the Shorty George at the Savoy. When her mother died, Ella's world changed and she was forced to live on the street. She still managed to wow the crowd at the famous Apollo Theater for Amateur Night. When she auditioned for the famous bandleader Chick Webb, Ella was too intimidated to sing, so she imagined she was singing for her mother instead. It wasn't long before Webb made her an official vocalist with the band. After three years, Ella wrote the words to a song that became a number-one hit on the radio: "A tisket, a tasket, / A brown and yellow basket."

Also highly recommended: *Ella Fitzgerald: The Tale of a Vocal Virtuosa.* By Andrea Davis Pinkney. Illustrated by Brian Pinkney. Jump at the Sun, 2002. 32 p. Ages 5–10. This picture book focuses on Ella's adulthood and is narrated by an anthropomorphic cat named Scat Cat Monroe.

Anne Frank

Anne Frank: The Anne Frank House Authorized Graphic Biography. By Sid Jacobson. Illustrated by Ernie Colón. Hill and Wang, 2010. 152 p. Ages 10–14.

This graphic novel biography begins before Anne Frank was born, covering her parents' lives. Panels parallel to Anne's story give a time line of events that led to the rise of the Nazis and other events that happened during World War II. In 1940, the Nazis invaded Denmark, where the Franks had fled to, and began operations at a concentration camp at Auschwitz. At the end of that year, Otto moved his business to a large building. "It even had an annex." For her birthday, Anne got a diary. Finally, the time came for Otto to hide his family and others in the secret annex. "And the diary was of course the first thing Anne packed." Miep Gies, one of the people who had helped the Franks, found Anne's diary after Anne and her family were arrested. After the war, Otto, the only survivor from those hiding in the annex, read Anne's entries and realized, "Never had I imagined the depths of her thoughts and feelings." He often replied to fans inspired by Anne's diary that they should "work for unity and peace."

Benjamin Franklin

Becoming Ben Franklin: How a Candle-Maker's Son Helped Light the Flame of Liberty. By Russell Freedman. Holiday House, 2013. 86 p. Ages 10–14.

Seventeen-year-old Ben ran away from his family and his apprenticeship in Boston and arrived in Philadelphia with "a Dutch dollar and about a shilling in copper." Ben went on to become a wealthy man after the publication of his book *Poor Richard's Almanack*. He accomplished much in life including establishing America's first lending library and inventing a wood-burning stove, known today as the Franklin stove. Ben's almanac made him rich, but it was his experiments with electricity that made him famous: "a couple of these experiments resulted in painful shocks, knocking him senseless." He and a friend mischievously rigged a portrait to shock anyone who touched it. His experiments with lightning became legendary. At this point in his life, Ben was known as possibly the biggest celebrity in America. This fame led to his recruitment to perform civic duties. Ben became deputy postmaster of the colonies; he established the first home-delivery service in America. He later had a role in America's independence from Great Britain. A French statesman said of Ben, "He snatched lightning from the sky and the scepter from tyrants."

Werner Franz

Surviving the **Hindenburg.** By Larry Verstraete. Illustrated by David Geister. Sleeping Bear Press, 2012. 40 p. Ages 5–10.

Werner was the youngest crew member of the famous *Hindenburg* zeppelin. At 804 feet, the aircraft was almost as long as the *Titanic* and as tall as a thirteen-story building. Werner was fourteen years old and spent his time doing chores for the officers and crew. He loved looking out of the small area in the bow of the ship, which allowed him a striking view of the Atlantic Ocean and, eventually, the skyscrapers of New York City. On May 6, 1937, the captain delayed landing due to bad weather. That evening, the *Hindenburg* was approaching the landing field in Lakehurst, New Jersey, when Werner heard "a muffled thud." Fire tore through the keel gangway and all around Werner. He remembered a small hatch used for bringing supplies into the *Hindenburg*. He kicked it open and jumped. Luckily, Werner landed on soft sand and ran to safety. Nobody on the ground knew he was from the *Hindenburg* until he managed to say, "*Ich bin der cabin-boy vom* Hindenburg!" The next morning, Werner located his grandfather's pocket watch in the wreckage. "Like Werner, it had survived the *Hindenburg*."

Wanda Gág

Wanda Gág: The Girl Who Lived to Draw. By Deborah Kogan Ray. Illustrated by the author. Viking, 2008. 40 p. Ages 5–10.

Wanda was the oldest of seven children growing up in New Ulm, Minnesota. She used her passion for drawing to earn money for the family. She sold some bookmarks and holiday cards, but worried when her art supplies ran low. *The Minneapolis Journal* hired Wanda to write and illustrate a serial story. She earned fifty dollars and also received a package of art supplies; she felt "the materials were like a gift from heaven." Wanda titled the story "Robby Bobby in Mother Goose Land." Wanda moved to New York City, where she won another scholarship to study art. At a gallery showing of her work, Wanda was approached by a children's book editor. "Children would love pictures that were filled with such a sense of wonder, she told Wanda—had she ever considered writing a story?" Wanda worked on one of her older manuscripts. That story turned out to be the popular book *Millions of Cats*. It went on to win a 1929 Newbery Honor Award. Many literary critics consider *Millions of Cats* to be the first modern American picture book.

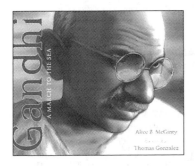

Mahatma Gandhi

Gandhi: A March to the Sea. By Alice B. McGinty. Illustrated by Thomas Gonzalez. Amazon, 2013. 40 p. Ages 7–12.

Gandhi thought British rule over India was wrong, particularly when Great Britain passed unfair laws. One law forbade Indians from taking salt from the ocean; instead, they were forced to buy salt from the British. Gandhi also felt it was wrong to solve problems with violence. With these thoughts in mind, Gandhi organized his famous twenty-four-day March to the Sea in 1930. He began his journey with seventy marchers. Thousands more—many of them poor—cheered on the sidelines. The marchers knew that with each step they took, they broke the law. Gandhi also visited the "Untouchables . . . outcasts of the Hindu faith," along the way. He told all of India that they must unite. Gandhi was joined by Muslims, Hindus, and untouchables, all taking "one more step toward freedom." When the marchers made it to the Arabian Sea, thousands gathered around Gandhi. Some of them were journalists sending the news around the world. Everyone wondered "if this small man leading this big fight can make things right." Gandhi scooped up salt. His followers did the same. "Never has salt tasted sweeter."

Maggie Gee
Sky High: The True Story of Maggie Gee. By Marissa Moss. Illustrated by Carl Angel. Tricycle Press, 2009. 32 p. Ages 5–10.

Maggie Gee was one of only two Chinese American women to serve in the Women Airforce Service Pilots (WASP) during World War II. When Maggie was a girl, her family would drive to airports to watch the planes fly. When the United States entered World War II, Maggie saw this as an opportunity to fly for her country. She took flying lessons and also taught herself how to drive a car to get to those lessons. She became a good enough pilot to be recruited by WASP. She learned to parachute, make emergency landings, and how "to loop the loop, and fly low over cows' heads, surprising them." Maggie earned her wings and joined male fighter pilots in training missions. Once, she made a scary landing in the dark. Another pilot was startled to see an Asian face; "I could tell that he was mistaking me for an enemy pilot, a Japanese kamikaze, or spy." Maggie assured him she was American "born and bred." She got back in her plane and "felt big and strong again, and no one could take that feeling away."

Althea Gibson
Nothing but Trouble: The Story of Althea Gibson. By Sue Stauffacher. Illustrated by Greg Couch. Knopf, 2007. 32 p. Ages 5–9.

Althea was a tall, wild tomboy from Harlem. Everyone said she was nothing but trouble. Althea didn't care what they thought. She loved sports: "Give her a stick, a paddle, a hoop, or a ball, and Althea Gibson was good to go." One day, a man named Buddy Walker saw potential in the girl who everyone else thought was trouble. Buddy scrounged enough money to buy Althea a secondhand tennis racket. She became very good at the sport. Several folks made arrangements for Althea to take formal tennis lessons. She wasn't very interested in game etiquette. After losing in her first real tennis tournament, Althea refused to shake the hand of her opponent. Instead, she tried to fight with someone in the grandstand. Althea eventually learned that her temper was harming her game. In time, tennis changed Althea, "but just as importantly . . . Althea changed tennis." She went on to become the first African American to compete in and win the Wimbledon Cup.

Jane Goodall
The Watcher: Jane Goodall's Life with the Chimps. By Jeanette Winter. Illustrated by the author. Schwartz & Wade Books, 2011. 40 p. Ages 5–10.

All of her life, little Valerie Jane Goodall was a keen observer of nature. She once fed a robin in her room; the robin felt so comfortable there that it built a nest in Jane's bookcase. As an adult, Jane finally realized her childhood dream of going to Africa. She started working for the famous scientist Louis Leakey, who was looking for someone to help study chimpanzees. In Tanzania, Jane lived in the wilderness. She felt at home there. She slowly built a relationship of trust with the chimps. Jane imitated their habits and became close to one particularly bold chimp she called David Greybeard. She discovered him using a stick as a tool to dig for termites: "Before this, nobody knew that wild animals made tools." Because of the danger from poachers and deforestation, the chimpanzees were headed toward extinction: "They needed Jane to speak for them." The author's notes mention that Jane referred to herself as the "white ape." Jane's own autobiographies are *My Life with the Chimpanzees* and *The Chimpanzees I Love: Saving Their World and Ours.*

Martha Graham
Martha Graham: A Dancer's Life. By Russell Freedman. Clarion, 1998. 176 p. Ages 12–14.

Martha Graham claims she never chose to become a dancer. Instead, she felt that she was chosen. She spent hours watching lions pace at the zoo and eventually learned "the inevitability of return, the shifting of one's body." As a child, she learned from her father that movement never lies. Martha's life changed when she watched professional dancer Ruth St. Denis perform. Even though many professional dancers begin formal training when they are nine or ten years old, Martha began at the age of twenty-two. She quickly became a rising star in Miss Ruth's school. At the age of thirty, she had developed her own personal dance style. She was inspired by the modern art movement: "I nearly fainted because at that moment I knew I was not mad, that others saw the world, saw art, the way I did . . . I said, 'I will do that someday. I will make dance like that.'" There were the critics, but as Martha stated, "I'd rather have them hate me than be indifferent to me." She went on to create 181 original dances, her last one composed in 1990 at the age of ninety-six.

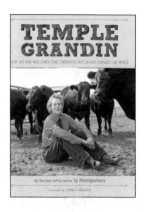

Temple Grandin

Temple Grandin: How the Girl Who Loved Cows Embraced Autism and Changed the World. By Sy Montgomery. Houghton Mifflin, 2012. 160 p. Ages 10–14.

Temple Grandin's autism is, as she says, "part of who I am." She became the leading authority on humane treatment of livestock. Temple faced a lot of discrimination while growing up, not only for her autism but also because of her gender. One section contains the offensive word *retard*. While the word directed at her stung, Temple gave it out as good as she received. She played pranks on the other girls, including hiding their school clothes during PE class so that they would have to spend the rest of the school day in their gym clothes. The chapter ends with Temple reacting to the girl's opening insult—by throwing a book at the girl and hitting her in the eye. Temple's family got a phone call later that day. "The headmaster of the school had called to say that she had been expelled from school." Another chapter showcases several students at Temple's new school, not "because of their problems but because of their abilities."

Gail Halvorsen

Candy Bomber: The Story of the Berlin Airlift's "Chocolate Pilot." By Michael O. Tunnell. Charlesbridge, 2010. 110 p. Ages 10–14.

U.S. Air Force pilot Gail Halversen helped with the 1948 Berlin Airlift. U.S. forces flew in food and supplies for the Berlin citizens. Gail toured the area one day and came upon a group of thirty German children on the other side of a fence. He slipped them four small pieces of gum and was amazed that there was no fighting. The children "ripped the wrappers into strips, passing them around so everyone could breathe in the sweet, minty smell." Gail told the kids to watch for his plane the next day because he would be dropping candy and gum from the air. He said, "When I get overhead, I'll wiggle the wings," to which one girl asked, "Vat is viggle?" Gail was able to meet several of the children years later. One of Gail's greatest memories was when he was asked to lead Germany's athletes in the opening of the 2002 Winter Olympic Games. One child told what it meant to get the chocolate from the sky: "It represented hope. Hope that someday we would be free. Without hope the soul dies."

Ruth Harkness

Mrs. Harkness and the Panda. By Alicia Potter. Illustrated by Melissa Sweet. Knopf, 2012. 40 p. Ages 4–10.

By 1934, few people in the Western world had seen a panda bear. William Harkness explored China hoping to bring a live panda back to the United States. When he died, his wife, Ruth, felt that she had "inherited an expedition." She was inspired to carry out his dream, even though people scoffed at her. Once Ruth arrived in China, "when a little girl waved three times, Mrs. Harkness took it as a sign of good luck." A man named Yang Di Lin helped Ruth travel the long distance to the mountain region to locate "*bei-shung*—the Chinese word for 'panda.'" They finally found a baby panda in a tree. Ruth named it Su Lin, which means "a little bit of something cute." The American newspapers heralded the arrival of Ruth and the baby panda with the headlines "Panda-monium!" The panda found a home at the Brookfield Zoo, outside of Chicago. The author's notes point out that the panda bear is the symbol of the World Wildlife Fund.

Ira Hayes

Quiet Hero: The Ira Hayes Story. By S. D. Nelson. Illustrated by the author. Lee & Low Books, 2006. 32 p. Ages 5–10.

Ira grew up on the Gila River Indian Reservation in Arizona. When he was nineteen, he joined the Marines. He bonded with the men in his battalion and, for the first time in his life, felt like he belonged somewhere. Ira fought in major battles across the Pacific Ocean. In 1945, the Marines landed on Iwo Jima, an important base for the Japanese. An American flag was planted at the top of Mount Suribachi to signal the end of Japanese control of the high ground. Ira and a small band of soldiers were then sent "to put up a bigger flag—one that could be seen for miles." A photographer caught them in action. "When people all across the United States saw the picture . . . they were awestruck. Tears came to the eyes of many." Ira was treated like a hero. Unfortunately, after the war, Ira became lonely and drank: "The drinks helped Ira cope with his feelings of being alone." He died in 1955 and was buried in Arlington National Cemetery, not too far from the large bronze statue that was created from that photograph—the United States Marine Corps War Memorial.

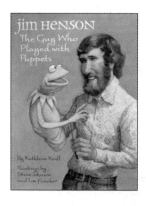

Jim Henson

Jim Henson: The Guy Who Played with Puppets. By Kathleen Krull. Illustrated by Steve Johnson and Lou Fancher. Random House, 2011. 32 p. Ages 5–10.

In the 1950s, when his family bought their first television set, young Jim became a fan of the puppet show *Kukla, Fran and Ollie.* To Jim, "playing with puppets seemed like a promising idea." Jim's first TV show, *Sam and Friends,* went on the air while he was still in college. He wanted to create puppets that were able to display several emotions; the Muppets were created. The word *Muppet* comes from a combination of *marionette* and *puppet.* The producers of a new show called *Sesame Street* called Jim. (The show's name came from the Arabian tale that used the phrase "Open Sesame" that was said to open a door to treasures; the producer wanted to "open doors in young minds.") Jim's company created characters such as Big Bird, Oscar the Grouch, Cookie Monster, and Bert and Ernie. In the 1970s, *The Muppet Show* was aired, "coaxing giggles from as many as 235 million people each week." After Jim passed away, Krull says, "with his vivid imagination—and playful way with puppets—Jim Henson had made a difference in this world."

Matthew Henson

Keep On! The Story of Matthew Henson, Co-Discoverer of the North Pole. By Deborah Hopkinson. Illustrated by Stephen Alcorn. Peachtree, 2009. 40 p. Ages 5–10.

There were few opportunities for a thirteen-year-old African American in the late nineteenth century. Matthew Henson begged for a job as a cabin boy and sailed around the world. His captain "taught him history and mathematics and soon Matt could navigate by the stars, tie sailor's knots, and fix or build most anything." There Matt met Robert E. Peary and joined him on an expedition to Greenland. Matt studied with the Inuit. He learned to hunt, fish, and build and drive a dogsled. Matt earned the nickname "*Mahri-Pahlik,* Matthew the Kind One." Quotes from Matt's autobiography are sprinkled throughout this book: "The wind would find the tiniest opening in our clothing and pierce us with the force of driving needles. Our hoods froze to our beards." The expedition made another attempt a few years later. Matt went through the ice one day in April 1909. He was saved by Ootah, one the Inuit explorers. A few days later,

Peary planted a flag on the spot on what they believed was the North Pole. Peary said, "Without Matt Henson there would be no Pole."

Hildegard
The Secret World of Hildegard. By Jonah Winter. Illustrated by Jeanette Winter. Scholastic, 2007. 64 p. Ages 7–10.

During the Middle Ages, "girls were not allowed to go to school, and most girls could not read. They were taught to serve and obey all the boys around them." In Germany, a girl named Hildegard was born. She saw a world invisible to other people. She kept those visions to herself; this caused her to have terrible headaches. Hildegard's parents sent her to live in a monastery. Years later, Hildegard was named the mistress of the monastery. She still had headaches, however, hiding her visions from others. She finally determined that God had visited her and instructed, "You must stop hiding my light. You must let other people see what *you* see." Her visions were written down, and her headaches went away. The pope approved of Hildegard, and she became known all over the land as a great preacher. "And when she had finished her work on this earth, her secret world kept shining, because she had the courage to let it shine."

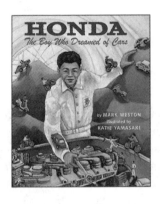

Soichiro Honda
Honda: The Boy Who Dreamed of Cars. By Mark Weston. Illustrated by Katie Yamasaki. Lee & Low Books, 2008. 32 p. Ages 5–10.

Soichiro Honda was amazed the first time he saw an automobile, a Ford Model T, drive through town. He later found work in a garage, sweeping and cleaning tools. He was upset that the owner told him, "DO NOT touch the cars!" After six years, Soichiro opened his own shop. He also designed racing cars, which he loved to drive at high speeds. He once was seriously hurt in an accident. He recovered and went on to invent a flexible piston ring. After World War II, Soichiro developed a motorized bicycle, and the Honda Motor Company was formed. He was a demanding boss, known as Mr. Thunder; on the other hand, he was also protective of his employees and created new jobs for them "when machines made their old jobs unnecessary." In 1959, Honda motorcycles were introduced to America. Their slogan was "You Meet the Nicest People on a Honda." The company next designed water-cooled engines for the Honda Civic, the first

Honda car sold in the United States. Most people today don't know Soichiro Honda, "but almost everyone knows his last name."

Harry Houdini

Escape! The Story of the Great Houdini. By Sid Fleischman. Greenwillow, 2006. 210 p. Ages 9–14.

Magic was Houdini's way to become "empowered and transformed." Houdini worked not only on his magic tricks, but also on his delivery to the audience, getting rid of his "dees, dem, and dose" patter. Houdini became the King of Handcuffs, breaking out of all shackle challenges. He developed bigger and more dangerous tricks—such as the Chinese Water Torture and the padlocked milk can trick—to keep the fickle audiences in awe. Houdini fought off imitators and debunked spiritualists, even though he was curious about the afterworld himself. At one point, the famous actress Sarah Bernhardt met Houdini. She had lost a leg and asked Houdini if he could bring back her leg for her. When he told her that it was impossible, Bernhardt replied, "Yes, but you do the impossible."

Also highly recommended: *Houdini: World's Greatest Mystery Man and Escape King.* By Kathleen Krull. Illustrated by Eric Velasquez. Walker, 2005. 36 p. Ages 5–12. This picture book biography shows Houdini's life in the form of a theatrical production.

William Hoy

Silent Star: The Story of Deaf Major Leaguer William Hoy. By Bill Wise. Illustrated by Adam Gustavson. Lee & Low Books, 2012. 34 p. Ages 5–10.

One day in 1889, center fielder William Hoy set a baseball major league record by throwing out three runners at home plate in one game. The fans of Hoy's team, the Washington Nationals, showed their appreciation by waving their handkerchiefs and hats in the air. "The fans made such a visual commotion because William Hoy was deaf." When William was three years old, he lost his hearing due to meningitis. He turned to baseball when he attended the Ohio School for the Deaf. While playing ball, William was spotted by the coach of a traveling amateur baseball team. William made the team but struggled at the plate. He worked out a system with his third-base coach, who signaled the home-plate umpire's calls so that William wouldn't have to turn around to face the ump and thus leave himself vulnerable to the pitcher's next throw. William finally made the big leagues, where a "sportswriter called him the best fielding outfielder in the National League." When William faced Luther Taylor, a young deaf pitcher, William signed, "I'm glad to see you!" After he got a base hit, William faced Taylor, who tipped his hat.

Dolores Huerta

Dolores Huerta: A Hero to Migrant Workers. By Sarah Warren. Illustrated by Robert Casilla. Marshall Cavendish, 2012. 32 p. Ages 5–10.

Biographer Warren lists the roles Dolores Huerta played in her life. "Dolores is a teacher." She noticed her students were sick, hungry, and poorly clothed. Dolores was a detective who talked to her students' parents. The parents replied that the bosses didn't pay the laborers enough money. Dolores was a friend who took a stand. Dolores was a warrior and confronted the bosses. Dolores was an organizer. She helped the workers form unions for better pay and conditions. Dolores was a storyteller who spread the word about the mistreatment of the workers. Dolores was a peacemaker. She used nonviolent ways to promote change. Dolores was a fortune-teller who predicted people wouldn't buy the produce when they learned how the workers were mistreated. The book comes full circle when we read once more, "Dolores is a teacher. She teaches people how to work as a team." *Ms. Magazine* named Dolores Huerta "Woman of the Year" in 1998, and President Clinton presented Dolores with the U.S. Presidential Eleanor D. Roosevelt Human Rights Award the same year.

Langston Hughes

Love to Langston. By Tony Medina. Illustrated by R. Gregory Christie. Lee & Low Books, 2002. 40 p. Ages 8–12.

Biographer Medina crafted fourteen poems that explore various aspects of poet Langston Hughes's life. The first poem, "Little Boy Blues," shows young Langston lamenting the fact that he can't go outside without the white kids making fun of the color of his skin. In the poem "First Grade," his teacher cruelly tells a white student not to eat licorice or he'll turn black like Langston. "Libraries" shows how important these institutions were to Langston: "To sit and to stay / with nooks and books / and books of endless / beautiful words / keeping me company / taking my loneliness / and blues / away." Langston traveled to Africa and other locations like "a miner searching for riches / from people of all races / discovering other voices and places." He also celebrated his home in Harlem: "Yeah, Harlem is where I be— / where I could be / Me / Harlem is the capital of my world." The back matter contains information behind each poem; share the corresponding background after you read each poem.

Clementine Hunter

Art from Her Heart: Folk Artist Clementine Hunter. By Kathy Whitehead.
Illustrated by Shane W. Evans. Putnam, 2008. 32 p. Ages 4–10.

Clementine worked on a plantation whose owner opened the house for artists
and writers. Clementine would wait until her chores were done well into the
evening before working on her art. She used leftover supplies such as window
shades and glass bottles. Clementine was self-taught. She drew pictures of the
world she knew—days of hard work, washing laundry and picking cotton.
Clementine also drew inspiration from the good times in her life—feeding
chickens, fishing, and spending time with her family. At last, Clementine put
up a sign that read "ART—EXHIBIT ADMISSION 25¢ THANKS" and hung her
artwork on a clothesline. Her fame spread, and soon she had a gallery in a New
Orleans museum. Ironically, she couldn't attend a showing of her own work at
the gallery at the Northwestern State College in Natchitoches, Louisiana,
because she was African American: "She had to wait until after hours to enjoy
her own pictures on display." The author's notes inform us that Clementine
received an honorary doctorate in fine arts in 1986 from the same institution
that didn't allow her to attend her own showing in 1955.

Zora Neale Hurston

Zora! The Life of Zora Neale Hurston. By Dennis
Brindell Fradin and Judith Bloom Fradin. Clarion, 2012.
180 p. Ages 12–14.

Zora was a natural storyteller from an early age. She
made a doll out of the outer covering of an ear of corn
and named her Miss Corn-Shuck. She also played
with Mr. Sweet Smell, a cake of soap, and Reverend
Door-Knob. Zora's mother encouraged her to "jump
at the sun. You might not land on the sun, but at least
you will get off the ground." Her idyllic life changed at the age of thirteen
when her mother passed away. Zora felt she was in "sorrow's kitchen." Zora
eventually moved to Harlem and became recognized for her writing talents.
Her books didn't sell many copies, and Zora was constantly broke. Once, she
didn't have the $1.83 to mail a manuscript to her publisher. She died penni-
less. Ironically, a new generation found her works, most notably her novel
Their Eyes Were Watching God, which sold millions of copies.

Also highly recommended: *Zora Hurston and the Chinaberry Tree.* By William
Miller. Illustrated by Cornelius Van Wright and Ying-Hwa Hu. Lee & Low Books,

1994. 32 p. Ages 4–10. Zora's bond with her mother is the focus of this picture book biography.

Huynh Quang Nhuong

The Land I Lost: Adventures of a Boy in Vietnam. By Huynh Quang Nhuong. HarperCollins, 1982. 127 p. Ages 8–12.

Quang Nhuong Huynh grew up in the central highlands of Vietnam. His hamlet consisted of bamboo houses surrounded by deep trenches to keep out bandits and dangerous creatures. "There were four animals we feared the most: the tiger, the lone wild hog, the crocodile, and the horse snake." Most of the fifteen short stories feature these and other animals, including his beloved water buffalo. In one story, his cousin captures a python snake by biting gently on its tail. "Never make the mistake of biting the python's tail too hard. If you did that, the python would get very angry and squeeze you to death." Other stories feature adventures with dogs, eels, monkeys, and otters. One nonanimal-related highlight is the chapter honoring his grandmother. She defeated a bully with her karate skills and drove away a group of bandits with a bow and arrow.

Also highly recommended: *Water Buffalo Days: Growing Up in Vietnam.* By Huynh Quang Nhuong. HarperCollins, 1997. 117 p. Ages 7–10. This companion autobiography focuses on the relationship between the author and Tank the water buffalo.

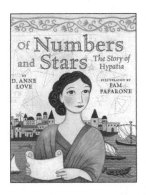

Hypatia

Of Numbers and Stars: The Story of Hypatia. By D. Anne Love. Illustrated by Pam Paparone. Holiday House, 2006. 32 p. Ages 5–10.

The city of Alexandria was a thriving center of learning in the fourth century. In a time when few girls had rights, Hypatia's father believed that "a girl should be educated in the same way as a boy." Hypatia became skilled in many areas, such as swimming, fishing, horseback riding, and rowing. She became particularly skilled in mathematics and philosophy. Word of her wisdom spread, and she herself taught many students. Following Hypatia's advice, one student named Synesius developed the astrolabe, an instrument to assist sailors "determine latitude and find true north as they journeyed across the sea." Hypatia became recognized as the most important woman philosopher during her time: "Through her extraordinary roles as scholar, philosopher, writer, and teacher, she became a symbol of learned women for centuries to come." The author's note in the back matter describes Hypatia's death. A patriarch of Alexandria supposedly urged fanatics to attack her. Perhaps he was fearful of her popularity or her refusal to embrace Christianity, or did it for political reasons. While scholars debate the actual reasons, we do know that no one was ever charged with the crime.

Ji-li Jiang

Red Scarf Girl: A Memoir of the Cultural Revolution. By Ji-li Jiang. HarperCollins, 1997. 285 p. Ages 10–14.

Sixth-grader Ji-li's world turned upside down in 1996 when Chairman Mao's Cultural Revolution was under way. She was a strong student, but the education system as a whole became vilified. Student turned against student; neighbor turned against neighbor. Ji-li's family was persecuted because her grandfather had been a landlord thirty years earlier. In one tense scene, the neighborhood Red Guard ransacked her family's apartment. "Home, I thought. Wasn't home a private place? A place where the family could feel secure? How could strangers come and search through our secrets?" Ji-li's father was arrested for the crime of listening to foreign radio. Ji-li was pressured to testify against both of her parents. "I would never do anything to hurt my family, and I would do everything I could to take care of them." In the author's notes, Ji-li talks about her flight to the United States with most of her family. She established her own company, the East West Exchange, to promote cultural awareness between American and China. "I hope this book will be part of that mission."

Joan of Arc

Joan of Arc. By Diane Stanley. Illustrated by the author. Morrow, 1998. 48 p. Ages 10–14.

When Joan was thirteen years old, she had the first of many visions. Saint Michael the Archangel and other saints convinced her to travel through enemy territory to see the crown prince Charles. Her father had other plans. He wanted her to marry and forbade her from traveling with soldiers. He told her brothers "that if Joan ever did such a scandalous thing, they should drown her." Joan followed her voices and convinced the proper authorities to send her to Charles. People across France looked upon her. Joan was given a suit of armor, and she became "the true heart and soul of the army." Joan took part in battles, and Charles was crowned king. The war continued, however, and Joan was eventually taken as prisoner. The outcome of the trial was predetermined; Joan was burned at the stake, "a dreadful way to die!" Many were distraught, and one Englishman cried, "We are all lost, for we have burnt a saint!" Joan was indeed made a saint by the Catholic Church approximately five hundred years after her death.

William Kamkwamba

The Boy Who Harnessed the Wind. By William Kamkwamba and Bryan Mealer. Illustrated by Elizabeth Zunon. Dial, 2012. 32 p. Ages 5–10.

William was curious how machines work. He thought about them as he worked in his father's fields in the African country of Malawi. A drought hit the region, and people began to starve. William found science books in a nearby library. He imagined building a windmill to produce electricity and pump water to the valley. "This windmill was more than a machine. It was a weapon to fight hunger." William gathered an assortment of metal pieces from the junkyard. He finally built a tower that resembled a wobbly giraffe. The wind came and turned the tower's blades. William connected wires and turned on a small lightbulb. He shouted, "Tonga! I have made electric wind!" He knew that with more work, the windmills could feed his people. The author's notes state that this drought occurred in 2001 and 2002. William's first tower produced electricity and was built with a tractor blade, a shock absorber, and the frame of a bicycle. William was fourteen years old at the time. A few years later, he built a windmill that pumped water.

Peg Kehret

Small Steps: The Year I Got Polio. By Peg Kehret. Whitman, 1996. 179 p. Ages 10–14.

Seventh-grader Peg developed three types of polio in 1949, including the most serious form: bulbar polio, which impairs one's ability to talk or swallow. One day, Peg woke up in a hospital paralyzed. After eight days of high temperature, and not being able to swallow anything but water and juice, Peg's parents brought her a milkshake. Despite the "no milk" and "no ice cream" orders, Peg got the shake down. "Within an hour, my temperature dropped. That chocolate milkshake may have saved my life." She got along with her physician, who even painted her toenails for her. Dr. Bevis told her that he wanted to see her walk. Peg, in turn, shared knock-knock jokes with him. "Knock, knock. Who's there? Wendy. Wendy who? Wendy toenails are painted, de patient gets well." After several months of therapy, Peg walked for Dr. Bevis. "Head up, shoulders back; heel, toe, heel, toe. Small steps."

Also highly recommended: *Animals Welcome: A Life of Reading, Writing, and Rescue.* Peg Kehret. Dutton, 2012. 175 p. Ages 8–12. Peg's second autobiography highlights the animals in her life after she and her husband turned their home into an animal rescue center.

Martin Luther King Jr.
Martin's Big Words: The Life of Martin Luther King, Jr. By Doreen Rappaport. Illustrated by Bryan Collier. Jump at the Sun, 2001. 32 p. Ages 5–10.

Martin Luther King Jr. decided as a child that he would use big words like the ones he heard his father preach. Martin also became a minister and taught the concepts of love and peace. "Sooner or later, all the people of the world will have to discover a way to live together." When Rosa Parks refused to give up her bus seat in 1955, Martin walked with Montgomery's black citizens until they were allowed to sit anywhere they wanted. Over the next ten years, Martin walked with others who fought for equal rights. He implored demonstrators to hold peaceful gatherings and avoid using violence. Martin won the Nobel Peace Prize because of his nonviolent practices. The lawmakers voted to end segregation. Although Martin was shot in 1968, "his big words are alive for us today."

Also highly recommended: *Marching to the Mountaintop: How Poverty, Labor Fights, and Civil Rights Set the Stage for Martin Luther King, Jr.'s Final Hours.* By Ann Bausum. National Geographic, 2012. 104 p. Ages 12–14. This biography for older readers focuses on the events that led up to King's assassination.

Margaret E. Knight
Marvelous Mattie: How Margaret E. Knight Became an Inventor. By Emily Arnold McCully. Illustrated by the author. Farrar, Straus and Giroux, 2006. 32 p. Ages 5–10.

Mattie drew sketches in a notebook labeled *My Inventions* when she was a young girl. She made whirligigs, jumping jacks, sleds, and kites for her brothers. After her mother and brothers got jobs at a textile mill, Mattie was intrigued by the workings of the machines. When she was twelve, Mattie started working in the mill too. She got up at 4:30 am and left work at 7:30 pm. One day, a factory worker—another young girl—got hit in the head by a piece of machinery. Mattie figured out what went wrong, drew pictures in her notebook, and showed them to the factory engineers. Mattie's ideas worked. When Mattie turned eighteen, she worked at a factory that made paper grocery bags. Mattie developed "a machine that could cut and glue a square-bottomed bag." Her idea was stolen by a man whose lawyer stated, "Miss Knight could not possibly understand the mechanical complexities of the machine." Mattie's notebook proved otherwise, and she "was a professional inventor for the rest of her life."

Issa Kobayashi

Cool Melons—Turn to Frogs! The Life and Poems of Issa. By Matthew Gollub. Illustrated by Kazuko G. Stone. Lee & Low Books, 1998. 40 p. Ages 6–12.

Issa's schoolmaster encouraged the boy to write haiku poems to express his feelings. Issa was very interested in nature: "Rest here / sleepy butterfly / I'll lend you my lap." After his mother died, Issa was raised by his grandmother: "Motherless sparrow / come play / with me." His father remarried and Issa's new stepmother turned out to be a mean person. Because Issa constantly argued with his stepmother, Issa's father sent him away. Issa found work with a master poet and then wandered the land for seven years, observing nature and finding pleasure in simple things: "A giant peony / rich and full / surely the God of Wealth dwells within." In his lifetime, this eighteenth-century Japanese poet wrote over twenty thousand haiku. Author Gollub mentions in the back matter how his translations changed the number of syllables from the original seventeen in order to keep the poems' "simplicity and charm." In addition to writing the biographical lines about Issa, author Gollub translated several of illustrators Stone's favorites for inclusion in this book. Both the English and Japanese words adorn each page.

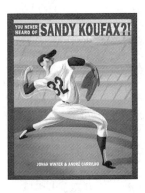

Sandy Koufax

You Never Heard of Sandy Koufax? By Jonah Winter. Illustrated by André Carrilho. Schwartz & Wade Books, 2009. 32 p. Ages 6–12.

A teammate of pitcher Sandy Koufax serves as the folksy narrator: "He was only the greatest lefty who ever pitched in the game of baseball." As a nineteen-year-old, Koufax was invited to become a member of the Brooklyn Dodgers baseball team, "and earnin' more dough than some of us old-timers." It was rough going for Koufax early in his career. He threw too hard and often lost control. He underwent a transformation and became a star player. Koufax refused to pitch the first game of the 1965 World Series because it fell on a

Jewish High Holy Day. He also surprised the baseball world when he retired at a young age. "Game after game, he throws so hard his elbow swells to the size of a grapefruit." The narrator concludes that Koufax's success was because he learned to relax his body enough to be a champion. "And what a thing of beauty that was."

Also highly recommended: *You Never Heard of Willie Mays?* By Jonah Winter. Illustrated by Terry Winder. Schwartz & Wade Books, 2012. 32 p. Ages 6–12. A fan tells us all about Willie Mays's accomplishments.

Jean Laffite
Jean Laffite: The Pirate Who Saved America. By Susan Goldman Rubin. Illustrated by Jeff Himmelman. Abrams, 2012. 48 p. Ages 8–12.

Jean's family was kicked out of Spain because of their Jewish heritage. When they were in their teens, Jean and his brother Pierre joined their older brother Alexander, who was already a pirate. Jean married a girl named Christine, and they raised their family in what is now Haiti. While sailing to France, Jean and his family were attacked by a Spanish man-of-war ship and marooned on an island. Even though they were rescued, Christine grew ill and died. Jean vowed revenge. Jean and his brothers moved to New Orleans. In 1807, after a fierce battle, Jean was finally able to avenge his wife's death. Jean became the leader of a group of pirates called the Baratarians. Governor Claiborne offered a reward of $500 for the capture of Jean. "With a good sense of humor, Jean responded by promising a reward of $5,000 for the capture of Governor Claiborne. Nothing came of it." Jean actually helped Claiborne during the War of 1812 by warning him of a British invasion on New Orleans. Jean became known as the Hero of New Orleans, "a pirate turned patriot."

Ruth Law
Ruth Law Thrills a Nation. By Don Brown. Illustrated by the author. Ticknor & Fields, 1993. 32 p. Ages 5–10.

On a cold November day in 1916, Ruth Law attempted to become the first person to fly an airplane from Chicago to New York in one day. For her adventure, she wore two woolen suits, two leather suits, and a skirt. Her airplane was a small air-show stunt plane. She had asked for a larger plane to be built, but the manufacturer refused her because he "did not believe a woman could fly a large plane." Ruth had a crude scroll of maps taped together and attached to her leg, plus a compass, a clock, and a speedometer to help set her course. As she arrived near Hornell, New York, Ruth ran out of gas and made an emergency landing. After she got a bite to eat at a local restaurant and her plane was refueled, Ruth took off again for New York City. Evening came and Ruth set down two hours away from her destination. She tied her plane to a tree and spent the night in Binghamton, New York. Ruth finished her trip in the morning.

Henrietta Leavitt
Look Up! Henrietta Leavitt, Pioneering Woman Astronomer. By Robert Burleigh. Illustrated by Raúl Colón. Simon & Schuster, 2013. 32 p. Ages 7–12.

All of her life, Henrietta stared at the night sky: "She wanted to know about the wonderful bigness of all she saw." Most of her classmates in astronomy courses were men. When she graduated from school in 1892, Henrietta got a job at an observatory. Unfortunately, she and other women working there recorded, measured, and calculated for long hours and poor pay. "The women were expected to 'work, not think.'" Henrietta kept studying the stars on her own time. She saw patterns no one else had considered. She impressed the head astronomer with her findings about a star's light power. "When astronomers know the true brightness of a star, it helps them figure out how far the star is from Earth." Because of Henrietta, astronomers learned that the Milky Way stretched farther than previously thought. New galaxies were also discovered. "The universe was far more vast than anyone had ever dreamed! The stars had spoken to Henrietta." The author's afterword mentions that one astronomer called Henrietta "one of the most important women ever to touch astronomy."

Sammy Lee
Sixteen Years in Sixteen Seconds: The Sammy Lee Story. By Paula Yoo. Illustrated by Dom Lee. Lee & Low Books, 2005. 32 p. Ages 7–12.

Korean American Sammy Lee couldn't swim at the public pool most days because of a "whites only" policy. On Wednesdays, people of color could use the pool. Sammy worked hard on becoming a good diver. When Sammy was eighteen, a man told him, "That's the lousiest dive I've ever seen!" That man, Jim Ryan, became Sammy's coach. Coach Ryan led Sammy through many hard drills, some of them in sandpits. Sammy graduated from high school with high honors but was angry that he couldn't attend prom because only white students could enter the auditorium where it was held. At the age of twenty-eight, Sammy competed at the 1948 Olympic Games held in London. "Here he was, the son of Korean immigrants, representing the United States at the Olympics." Sammy won a bronze medal and performed a dangerous move in another diving event. "He had trained sixteen years for this—a moment that would last barely sixteen seconds from the time he dived to when the scores would be revealed." Sammy Lee became the first Asian American to win an Olympic gold medal.

Clara Lemlich

Brave Girl: Clara and the Shirtwaist Makers' Strike of 1909. By Michelle Markel. Illustrated by Melissa Sweet. Balzer & Bray, 2013. 32 p. Ages 5–10.

Young Clara Lemlich, all of five feet, immigrated to the United States and found a factory job making women's clothing. Clara and the other girls were locked inside the factory and ordered to work faster and faster by the bosses. "The sunless room is stuffy from all the bodies crammed inside. There are two filthy toilets, one sink, and three towels for three hundred girls to share." The workers lost pay or were sometimes fired for the smallest offenses, such as arriving a few minutes late or pricking their finger and getting a drop of blood on the cloth. Clara helped organize a strike to improve working conditions; the bosses retaliated by hiring men to beat the strikers. Clara was arrested seventeen times during the walkout. "They break six of her ribs, but they can't break her spirit. It's shatterproof." The bosses gave in and allowed the workers to form unions. The biography ends with the line, "Warriors can wear skirts and blouses, and the bravest hearts may beat in girls only five feet tall."

Ida Lewis

The Bravest Woman in America. By Marissa Moss. Illustrated by Andrea U'Ren. Tricycle Press, 2011. 32 p. Ages 5–10.

Ida felt like the luckiest girl in the world when her father got a job as a lighthouse keeper. Ida learned how to row and, over the years, felt the oars were a part of her. She also learned how to maintain the lighthouse's light, "how to fill it with oil, trim the wick, and clean the lens." When her father became ill, Ida kept watch. One cold evening, she spotted a small boat that pitched and tossed four boys into the rough water. Ida quickly rowed out to them. "Their legs churned the water in panic, their clothes weighed them down in the slapping waves, and the icy cold of the water made them gasp for breath." Ida kept her cool and pulled them onto her boat one by one. One of the boys passed out, but Ida rowed them to safety. Afterward, her father gave her his captain's hat:

"Ida was in charge of the lighthouse now." The author's afterword informs us that Ida officially rescued eighteen lives and possibly more during her tenure. She received a Congressional Life Saving Medal in 1874.

Li Cunxin

Dancing to Freedom: The True Story of Mao's Last Dancer. By Li Cunxin. Illustrated by Anne Spudvilas. Walker, 2007. 40 p. Ages 5–10.

Li Cunxin (lee schwin-sing) grew up very poor in a northern Chinese village. His father told him the story of a frog that lived at the bottom of a well. The frog tried to hop out to see the world, but the frog's father said that it was no use. He had already "tried all my life to get out." He kept thinking about this story as his parents worked hard to feed their family. One day, officials came to his school looking for candidates to study ballet. Eleven-year-old Li Cunxin was chosen and taken miles away from his family to a large city. By the time he was eighteen, he was recognized as one of the best dancers in China and offered a chance to study ballet in America. He became an international star. His highlight came when his parents were flown from China to see him dance in *The Nutcracker*: "My heart soared with happiness and I danced the dance of my life."

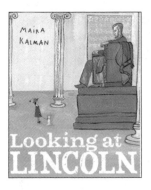

Abraham Lincoln

Looking at Lincoln. By Maira Kalman. Illustrated by the author. Nancy Paulsen Books, 2012. 32 p. Ages 5–10.

A young girl spots a tall bearded man and realizes that he reminds her of Abraham Lincoln. She heads to the library and learns many aspects of Lincoln's life. The girl shares these tidbits of knowledge—for example, the Lincoln family owned a dog named Fido and Abe always had apples on his desk. The girl asks many questions: Did his wife, Mary, make Abe a vanilla cake the day he was elected president? The girl learned that Mary made one when they were courting. Did Abe think about what kind of birthday present to buy his son? "Maybe a whistle or pickup sticks." The girl concludes that Abe loved people and that he wanted justice and freedom for all. She states that he lives on forever. As the girl approaches the Lincoln Memorial in Washington, DC, she says, "You can look into his beautiful eyes. Just look."

Also highly recommended: *Lincoln: A Photobiography.* By Russell Freedman. Clarion, 1987. 150 p. Ages 8–14. This Newbery Award winner covering Lincoln's life set the standard for modern-day biographies for young people.

Charles Lindbergh
Flight: The Journey of Charles Lindbergh. By Robert Burleigh. Illustrated by Mike Wimmer. Philomel, 1991. 32 p. Ages 5–10.

In 1927, Charles attempted the first solo airplane flight of 3,600 miles from New York to Paris, France. To make his plane light enough to carry the right amount of fuel, Charles had to leave behind his radio and parachute. Charles kept a diary of his journey. As he passed over icebergs, he wrote, "White pyramids . . . White patches on a blackened sea; sentries of the Arctic." At night, Charles ran into a storm. He tried to fly above it, but ice formed on the wings and forced him back into turbulent conditions. Paris was still two thousand miles away. "His body cries for sleep. He loses track of time." At last, after a little more than thirty-three hours, his plane landed. There's no time for Charles to rest, yet. He is greeted by thousands of well-wishers. Finally, after sixty hours, Charles goes to bed. "When he wakes, his life will be changed forever."

Also highly recommended: *Charles A. Lindbergh: A Human Hero.* By James Cross Giblin. Clarion, 1997. 212 p. Ages 12–14. This complete biography of Lindbergh's life shows that he was an "all-too-human hero" with "his share of weaknesses, along with tremendous strengths."

Belva Lockwood
Ballots for Belva: The True Story of a Woman's Race for the Presidency. By Sudipta Bardhan-Quallen. Illustrated by Courtney A. Martin. Abrams, 2008. 32 p. Ages 5–10.

Belva had a hard time finding a law school that would admit her. One rejection letter told her that women would distract the male students. Belva found one school that did indeed admit women. However, the fifteen women enrolled were not allowed to "go to the same classes as the men or to take their exams in the same rooms." Twelve of the women dropped out. Belva finished her coursework but was denied her diploma. She convinced President Ulysses S. Grant to intercede on her behalf and became the first woman to graduate from National University Law School. Belva was the first woman to argue a case before the U.S. Supreme Court. In 1884, she became the first woman to officially run for the president of the country, against Grover Cleveland and James

Blaine. Women couldn't vote, but nothing prevented them from running for office. (Still, Belva couldn't legally vote for herself.) After the election, it was revealed that several ballots cast for Belva were thrown away or given to the other candidates. Despite the struggles she faced, Belva knew "she had moved that mountain as far as it would go at the time."

Konrad Lorenz

The Goose Man: The Story of Konrad Lorenz. By Elaine Greenstein. Illustrated by the author. Clarion, 2009. 32 p. Ages 4–10.

Konrad observed geese his whole life in Austria. He became a medical doctor but decided instead to follow his passion, specializing in observing wildlife. Konrad studied newly hatched goslings and interpreted the different sounds they made: "He had watched enough geese to know that the sound meant 'I'm lost,' and he knew what to chirp back to calm her." One day, when a gosling followed him, he knew "the baby goose had decided that *he* was her parent." Konrad named that bird Martina. Everywhere Konrad went, Martina followed. Konrad's wife "just shook her head and put up with the mess the goose made." One day, a second goose arrived. Konrad named him Martin. After the two geese eventually flew away, Konrad experimented with other hatchlings. Geese followed him all over. Sometimes he slept outside with the geese. Konrad went on to win an important prize for his work with geese. The author's notes let us know that prize turned out to be the Nobel Prize for Konrad's work with bird instincts, including imprinting, "which means attaching itself to the first thing it sees."

Joe Louis

A Nation's Hope: The Story of Boxing Legend Joe Louis. By Matt de la Peña. Illustrated by Kadir Nelson. Dial, 2011. 40 p. Ages 6–12.

This biography, told in verse, opens with the 1938 boxing match of Joe Louis vs. Max Schmelling. "All witness the most important / match in boxing history / Soft-spoken Joe Louis against the one man / who put him on his back." Joe knew there was a lot at stake: the perception of the son of a sharecropper against a representative of Hitler's Nazis. As the bell rings, the narrative shifts to Joe's early life, when he was ridiculed for his stammering. Joe began working out at the local gym, getting knocked down quickly during his first amateur fight. He listened to the older boxers and "grew into his body." The boxing ring became his home. He knocked his opponent out of the ring in his first professional match. Joe became a hero to African Americans. In his first fight against Schmelling, Joe was knocked down. "Harlem streets struck silent." As news of the German concentration camps came out, all of America, white and black, needed a hero. Back at the ring, Joe struck first. Schmelling went down and again, a second time. "Just like that it's over / Joe has shocked the world."

Nat Love

Best Shot in the West: The Adventures of Nat Love. By Patricia C. McKissack and Fredrick L. McKissack Jr. Illustrated by Randy DuBurke. Chronicle, 2012. 132 p. Ages 10–14.

African American cowboy Nat Love's story is told in graphic novel format. He grew up a slave and after receiving his freedom, headed out West to become a cowpuncher. Nat became an expert at breaking in horses. On the range, he realized that the men were expendable, but the cattle under their watch were valuable. Nat became fearless and smart; "I also learned how to be dangerous." His reputation grew as he won a roping contest and then a shooting competition. The rules for the latter were to take fourteen shots with a rifle and hit targets a hundred yards away and then another fourteen shots from 250 yards. "The bull's-eye was about the size of an apple. I got all twenty eight on target." Nat goes on to recount his encounters with Bat Masterson and Billy the Kid. When captured by Yellow Dog's tribe, Nat asked his captors if they were going to make him a slave. He declared, "I'd rather die fighting than go back to that life."

Juliette Gordon Low

Here Come the Girl Scouts! The Amazing All-True Story of Juliette "Daisy" Gordon Low and Her Great Adventure. By Shana Corey. Illustrated by Hadley Hooper. Scholastic, 2012. 40 p. Ages 4–10.

Daisy was encouraged to be a delicate lady, but she responded to this by saying, "Bosh! How boring!" Daisy became inspired by the Boy Scouts and Girl Guides groups in England. She thought American girls should have a similar organization. In 1912, Daisy invited eighteen girls to the first Girl Scout meeting. She and a friend wrote a handbook that taught girls fascinating things, such as how to stop a runaway horse and "how to secure a burglar with eight inches of cord." The girls camped out too—"they sang songs around the campfire. They feasted on fish and cornbread and turtle eggs." New Girl Scout troops spread all over the nation, and girls of all races and class were invited to join. The biography ends with portraits of famous Girl Scouts, including basketball star Rebecca Lobo, actress Lucille Ball, and politician Hilary Clinton.

Also highly recommended: *First Girl Scout: The Life of Juliette Gordon Low.* By Ginger Wadsworth. Clarion, 2012. 210 p. Ages 11–14. This complete biography shows how Juliette Low found purpose in her life by establishing America's Girl Scouts.

Maritcha Rémond Lyons
Maritcha: A Nineteenth-Century American Girl. By Tonya Bolden. Abrams, 2005. 48 p. Ages 10–14.

New York City in 1848, the year of Maritcha Lyons's birth, "was a hustle-bustle, high-strung place of extremes: shack-and-rags poverty amid colossal wealth; virulent vice (gambling, drunkenness, brawls) alongside virtuous living." Maritcha's parents were free at a time when many African Americans in the South were still enslaved. The two were active in helping with the Underground Railroad. When a riot broke out in New York City, Maritcha's home was destroyed. Her family had to flee, and they resettled in Providence, Rhode Island. Maritcha had to fight for a seat at school because "there was no high school for blacks." She was allowed to attend but "the iron had entered my soul. I never forgot that I had to sue for the privilege which any but a colored girl could have without asking." She often wrote school papers on topics such as slavery, the Underground Railroad, and the New York City draft riots. Her teachers asked her if everything was true or if her imagination was running away with her. Maritcha replied that she was writing about the real-life events that weren't being taught. In 1869, Maritcha became the first African American to graduate from Providence High School.

Wangari Maathai
Seeds of Change: Planting a Path to Peace. By Jen Cullerton Johnson. Illustrated by Sonia Lynn Sadler. Lee & Low Books, 2010. 40 p. Ages 5–10.

Wangari grew up learning the importance of trees in her homeland of Kenya. When she finished elementary school, she moved to the city, away from her family. "At night when the girls slept, Wangari dreamed of home and the sweet figs of the mugumo trees. Her dreams reminded her to honor her Kikuyu tradition of respecting all living things." She eventually came to the United States and became a biologist. Wangari returned home and was dismayed to see the deforestation done by foreign companies to clear land for coffee plantations. She taught her countrywomen how to plant trees. She was arrested at one point because a corrupt businessman was upset with her Green Belt movement. In time, Wangari became known as "Mother of Trees" and won the Nobel Peace Prize in 2004. She continues to spread the message she learned as a young girl, that "persistence, patience, and commitment—to an idea as small as a seed but as tall as a tree that reaches for the sky—must be planted in every child's heart."

Dolley Madison

Dolley Madison Saves George Washington. By Don Brown. Illustrated by the author. Houghton Mifflin, 2007. 32 p. Ages 5–10.

Dolley Madison was very popular: "Everybody loves Mrs. Madison. That's because Mrs. Madison loves everybody." She married James Madison and "joined his hectic political life." Dolley became a leading hostess for President Thomas Jefferson and then for her husband when he became president of the United States. In 1814, Britain invaded America. The British army approached Washington, DC, and "the one hundred soldiers that were supposed to be guarding the presidential mansion ran off." But Dolley stayed behind. She had two servants unscrew the large portrait of George Washington; she didn't want it destroyed by the English soldiers. The servants had to chop the frame apart with a hatchet to free the painting from the wall. Dolley fled as "the city of Washington burned," disguising herself "as a simple farm woman," before finally reuniting with James. Months later, after the war ended, Dolley went back to being a busy hostess. She was friends with many important leaders, "including the first eleven presidents." The book ends with the information that the painting of Washington survived thanks to Dolley Madison and is on display at the White House to this day.

Jack Mandelbaum

Surviving Hitler: A Boy in the Nazi Death Camps. By Andrea Warren. HarperCollins, 2001. 146 p. Ages 12–14.

Fifteen-year-old Jack, who grew up in Poland, faced a horrendous moment when he, his mother, and brother were seized by the Nazis. Jack was separated from them, and he never saw his family again. He was taken to a camp, where his skin was cleansed with a burning solution, his head was shaven, and he was assigned his new identity—the number 16013. Jack's guards believed their Jewish prisoners were subhuman and deserved to be punished. A fellow prisoner told Jack to think of his survival as a game: "Play the game right and you might outlast the Nazis." Jack woke up with dysentery and was taken to the sick barracks. He noticed a doctor going around giving prisoners shots. They immediately died, so Jack staggered out. Another prisoner got him safely back to his bunk. When he was finally liberated, Jack was eighteen years old and weighed eighty pounds. Jack made it to the United States, where he became a successful businessman. He states that he survived because he "did not allow Hitler to make me feel less than human."

Effa Manley

She Loved Baseball: The Effa Manley Story. By Audrey Vernick. Illustrated by Don Tate. HarperCollins, 2010. 32 p. Ages 5–10.

Effa Brooks was scolded by her first-grade teacher for playing with African American children. The teacher didn't realize "those negroes" were Effa's siblings: "While Effa's skin was light, like her mother's, her siblings were dark, like their father." Effa couldn't make sense of the prejudicial feelings some people had. She and her husband, Abe, started the Brooklyn Eagles baseball team for the new Negro National League in 1935. She was good at her job handling the team's business. To the players, she became affectionately known as "mother hen." Her proudest moment came when the Eagles won the 1946 Negro League World Series. The next year, Jackie Robinson became the first black player in the major leagues. As a result, the Negro League started losing many of their best players. In the 1970s, Effa started a campaign to recognize several players from the now defunct Negro League for the National Baseball Hall of Fame. After a hard struggle, she succeeded once again. Years after her death, she became the first woman inducted into the Hall of Fame.

Juan Francisco Manzano

The Poet Slave of Cuba: A Biography of Juan Francisco Manzano. By Margarita Engle. Holt, 2006. 183 p. Ages 10–14.

Biographer Engle portrays the cruel life of Juan Manzano through a series of poems narrated by Juan himself, his natural parents, his owners, the son of an owner, and an overseer. Juan was born in Cuba in 1797 to a wealthy woman who claimed him as her own son. When she died, Juan was given to a cruel woman who punished him over and over again for the slightest offenses: "Every time I catch him reading / under a table / or behind a door / I lock him down in the cellar / with the charcoal / to darken his thoughts / and his skin." She failed to break Juan's spirit. Juan was also whipped several times. Through it all, Juan developed a love of learning and a talent of poetry. "My mind is a brush made of feathers/ painting pictures of words." He finally escaped his torturous life by fleeing on horseback. As he rode, he thought he heard many voices, from slaves and those who are free. "Many languages/ from Africa/ and all the various/ dialects of Spain/ many voices/ praying for me."

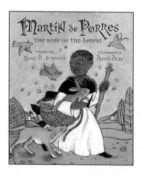

Martin de Porres, Saint

Martin de Porres: The Rose in the Desert. By Gary D. Schmidt. Illustrated by David Diaz. Clarion, 2012. 32 p. Ages 5–10.

A young African former slave brought her newborn baby to a priest in Peru to be baptized. "'Who is this child?' asked the priest. 'He is a rose in the desert,' said Anna." She named her child Martin. The boy grew up in the barrios, "where the slaves and poorest Indians lived." His father, a Spanish royal conqueror, came into Martin's life long enough to take him out of the barrios. Martin was apprenticed to a *cirujano,* a surgeon, to learn how to "take out teeth, to bleed a patient with leeches, to set broken bones, and to cut hair." A man whom Martin healed gave the boy lemon seeds as a gift. The tree grew the next morning and gave fruit spring, summer, fall, and winter. Word spread about Martin's healing powers and miracles. When he was fifteen, Martin worked at a monastery and continued sharing his gifts. The Spanish royalty also asked for Martin's services. "And they learned to wait for him to tend to the poorest among the barrios first." Martin became the first black saint in the Americas.

Lulu McLean

The Silent Witness: A True Story of the Civil War. By Robin Friedman. Illustrated by Claire A. Nivola. Houghton Mifflin, 2005. 32 p. Ages 5–10.

Four-year-old Lulu McLean lived on a plantation in Manassas, Virginia. It was 1861, the beginning of the Civil War. Confederate General Beauregard used the McLean home as headquarters. Once, a cannonball tore in the kitchen. "It exploded in a pot of stew that was supposed to be General Beauregard's lunch. Nobody was hurt." The ensuing fight became the first major battle of the war. The McLean family moved to Appomattox Court House. Lulu and her family "used raspberry leaves to make tea and burnt corn to make coffee." When the war neared its ending, Generals Lee and Grant walked into the room of the house where Lulu was playing. Lulu fled the room, leaving her rag doll behind on the sofa. After the surrender, the soldiers called Lulu's doll their "silent witness" to the event. One lieutenant colonel took the doll as a souvenir, and Lulu never saw it again. The doll now resides at the Appomattox Court House National Historic Park. Lulu's father "could rightfully say, 'The war started in my front yard and ended in my front parlor.'"

Joseph Medicine Crow

Counting Coup: Becoming a Crow Chief on the Reservation and Beyond. By Joseph Medicine Crow. National Geographic, 2006. 128 p. Ages 9–14.

Joseph was born in 1913 and grew up on the Crow Indian Reservation in southeastern Montana. He describes the various schools he attended; he had little success at some of the schools due to cultural differences between the white teachers and the other Native American students. He became the first male Crow Indian to graduate from college. The title refers to the custom that a Crow warrior had to perform four different types of war deeds, four "'coups,'" in order to become a chief." These deeds include sneaking into an enemy camp and capturing a horse, touching the first enemy to fall in battle, taking away an enemy's weapon, and finally, leading a successful war party. "There were no shortcuts. Each coup involved risking one's life." Joseph became an American soldier in World War II. At one point, Joseph had stolen horses that belonged to Hitler's SS officers. He didn't realize it at the time, but when Joseph returned home and told his war stories to the elders, they pointed out that "lo and behold, I had completed the four requirements to become a chief."

Florence Mills

Harlem's Little Blackbird: The Story of Florence Mills. By Renée Watson. Illustrated by Christian Robinson. Random House, 2012. 40 p. Ages 4–9.

When a thunderstorm passed over little Florence's house, she sang until the storm went away. "If my voice is powerful enough to stop the rain, what else can it do?" Florence was invited to sing in a fancy theater, but the manager said her friends couldn't attend because of the "whites only" policy. Florence refused to sing, so the manager relented. Florence was excited when she was invited to perform overseas, but "when she boarded the ship, the white passengers refused to eat in the same dining room as Florence and her troupe." Even so, she became an international star and wondered, "If my voice can take me around the world, what else can it do?" Florence's signature tune was "I'm a Little Blackbird Looking for a Bluebird." She felt the song was a cry for civil rights. She also became known for her generosity. When Florence passed away at a young age in 1927, over 150,000 people gathered in Harlem. Biographer Watson remarks that hundreds of blackbirds also came. Duke Ellington was so inspired by her voice that he wrote the song "Black Beauty" in her honor.

Jackie Mitchell

The Baseball Adventure of Jackie Mitchell, Girl Pitcher vs. Babe Ruth. By Jean L. S. Patrick. Adapted by Emma Carlson Berne. Illustrated by Ted Hammond and Richard Pimentel Carbajal. Graphic Universe, 2011. 32 p. Ages 5–12.

Seventeen-year-old female pitching sensation Jackie Mitchell is featured in this graphic novel biography. She signed a contract with the Chattanooga Lookouts, a men's semiprofessional baseball team, in 1931. They were scheduled to play a preseason game against the New York Yankees. Jackie knew every batter had a weakness and was very confident. Still, while warming up before the big game, Jackie worried about her "drop pitch." Because of the cool air, it was harder for her to control this special pitch. Finally, it was time for her to pitch to the mighty Babe Ruth. Strike one. Jackie decided to throw a high fastball. Strike two. Her third pitch had "some smoke on it" and she did it. Jackie struck out Ruth, the most famous baseball player of the time. "Four thousand fans screamed and jumped to their feet." According to the author's notes, Jackie received lots of fan mail. Unfortunately, the head of professional baseball nullified her contract and banned women from playing professional baseball—"but fans still talk about her strikeouts."

Anne Carroll Moore

Miss Moore Thought Otherwise: How Anne Carroll Moore Created Libraries for Children. By Jan Pinborough. Illustrated by Debby Atwell. Houghton Mifflin, 2013. 40 p. Ages 5–10.

At one time, many librarians frowned at the thought of children in public libraries. They wouldn't "let children touch the books, for fear that would smudge their pages or break their spines. They thought if children were allowed to take books home, they would surely forget to bring them back." Annie Moore changed that. She got a job at the Pratt Free Library in New York City. She opened a special room for children, often reading to them. Annie took down the signs that said SILENCE and had the children follow a pledge to take good care of the books. She wrote book reviews, made recommended book lists for parents, and corresponded with publishers to ensure they published quality children's books. When a new library was built on Fifth Avenue and Forty-Second Street in 1911, Annie made sure the children's room was spectacular. She had child-size chairs and tables made and artwork hanging on the walls—and, of course, shelves filled with "the best children's books she could find." Crowds of people attended opening day, including President William Howard Taft. Libraries all over the world followed Miss Moore's model and created their own special places for children.

Agnes Morley
Basketball Belles: How Two Teams and One Scrappy Player Put Women's Hoops on the Map. By Sue Macy. Illustrated by Matt Collins. Holiday House, 2011. 32 p. Ages 5–10.

Agnes Morley boasted that "nobody can ever accuse me of being a girly-girly." She attended Stanford University and joined the women's basketball team. On April 4, 1896, Stanford played Berkeley in the first women's intercollegiate basketball game. There were no men in the stands: "Our opponents from Berkeley don't feel it's proper for women to perspire in front of men." Instead, the teams played for "more than five hundred ladies cheering at the top of their lungs." Near the end of the game, both teams committed fouls. A player from each team got to shoot a foul shot. After the Berkeley player missed, Agnes's teammate Frances took Stanford's turn. "It flies toward the basket . . . and drops right in." Stanford went on to win by a score of 2–1. Biographer Macy uses Morley's first-person perspective to give a detailed account of the game. "What a sight we all are! Our hair is messy. Our bloomers are torn. Our faces are streaked with sweat. This might not be what my mother had in mind when she sent me to Stanford to become a lady."

Maria Anna Mozart
For the Love of Music: The Remarkable Story of Maria Anna Mozart. By Elizabeth Rusch. Illustrated by Steve Johnson and Lou Fancher. Tricycle Press, 2011. 32 p. Ages 5–10.

Maria was a skilled musician and composer. When she played, "notes fluttered out like a fountain, like raindrops on a puddle, like a warm wind." Her little brother, Wolfgang, was fascinated by her playing. He learned to play himself, and the two were called "Wonders of Nature! Child Geniuses!" The two played before royalty all across Europe. At the age of twelve, Maria was acknowledged as one of the continent's best pianists. When Wolfgang composed his first symphony, Maria wrote it down for him. Wolfgang knew that at the piano, his sister was his equal. Wolfgang continued traveling; Maria was heartbroken to be left behind. Eventually, she married and took care of five stepchildren. She made time each day to play music. Maria mourned when Wolfgang died at a young age. When she was older, she was delighted by a visitor—Wolfgang's son. "Together, she and Wolfgang's son played and played, for the love of music." The biography is broken up into small segments of text, each given the heading of a different musical term.

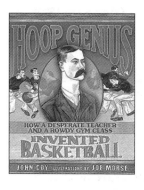

James Naismith

Hoop Genius: How a Desperate Teacher and a Rowdy Gym Class Invented Basketball. By John Coy. Illustrations by Joe Morse. Carolrhoda, 2013. 32 p. Ages 5–10.

"In December of 1891, James Naismith, a young teacher, took over a rowdy gym class that had already forced two teachers to quit." The students themselves were bored with the exercises and gymnastics they were forced to do. James hated the thought of giving up. He recalled a time when he was as energetic and eager for excitement as these boys. He had a moment of inspiration: an arcing throw requiring accuracy could be the cornerstone of a brand-new game. He grabbed a soccer ball, the school building superintendent contributed two peach baskets, and the rules of this new game were posted on a bulletin board. Many fouls were called that first game, but one twenty-five-foot shot went through "for the first and only basket of the game." Word spread, and eventually the game of basketball became an Olympic sport in 1936. "James Naismith attended the opening ceremonies, and when each nation dipped its flag to honor him, tears of happiness came to his eyes." The last illustration shows ghostly images of James and his gym class students watching a modern-day basketball game.

Manjira Nakahama

Shipwrecked! The True Adventures of a Japanese Boy. By Rhoda Blumberg. HarperCollins, 2001. 80 p. Ages 8–14.

Manjira joined a fishing crew to help support his family in Japan. When his ship got caught in a storm, "the fishermen felt as though they had fallen off the edge of the earth, for they could see nothing but sky and sea." After a week of bad weather, they arrived at a deserted island three hundred miles from their home. The men made headquarters in a cave and subsisted on seaweed, shellfish, and albatross. They were finally rescued by an American whaling vessel five months later. Manjira stayed on and learned how to navigate the whaling ship. Because of Japan's isolation policy, Manjira was reputed to be the first Japanese man to set foot in the United States. His new country baffled him. He noted strange American customs such as "a man sits on a chair instead of a floor." Manjira was homesick for Japan, but when he finally made it back, he was arrested for being a foreigner. After six months in prison, Manjira was reunited with his family—almost twelve years since the great storm took him away. Manjira went on to become a samurai and helped Japan join the modern world.

Tenzing Norgay

Tiger of the Snows: Tenzing Norgay: The Boy Whose Dream Was Everest. By Robert Burleigh. Illustrated by Ed Young. Atheneum, 2006. 32 p. Ages 7–10.

The mountain called to the young Sherpa boy Tenzing, who grew up in its shadow. Biographer Burleigh writes in verse format. "A song for Tenzing / Tenzing Norgay / Pathfinder / Hungry for the taste of clouds." Tenzing "studied the lore of the axe / And apprenticed himself to death and danger." On May 29, 1953, Tenzing and Edmund Hillary approached the top of the mountain. At dawn—with one thousand feet to go and the temperature registering seventeen below—the two, roped together, climbed into the Zone of Death. Their arms felt like tree trunks, their feet felt like lead, and they hungrily gulped for air. They finally reached the top, the first two men ever to do so. Tenzing embraced Hillary and unfurled four flags. The author's notes mentions that the flags represented the United Nations, India, Great Britain, and Nepal. Tenzing felt both joy and sadness. They could only spend a few moments before turning back. However, Tenzing knew that a part of him would remain at the peak. "Mountain / Chomolungma, I am with you / I am with you always."

Annie Oakley

Bull's-Eye: A Photobiography of Annie Oakley. By Sue Macy. National Geographic, 2001. 64 p. Ages 10–14.

Phoebe Ann's sisters nicknamed her Annie. She helped her family by hunting with her late father's rifle. "'I don't know how I acquired the skill,' she once said. 'I suppose I was born with it.'" When she was fifteen, Annie entered a shooting contest and beat her opponent, Frank Butler, on the last shot. "She won the contest, and in the process, she also won Frank's heart." The two got married and became shooting partners, performing trick shots for paying audiences. Annie took the stage name Annie Oakley. The couple wanted to be in Buffalo Bill's Wild West show, so Annie practiced before her tryout. Frank launched clay pigeons, and Annie "hit them with her shotgun held right side up, upside down, in her left hand, and in her right." Buffalo Bill's partner was watching and hired her on the spot. Annie became an international star and traveled all over America and Europe. After Annie and Frank retired from the road, she continued to have an active social life, donated money and her time to charities, and gave shooting demonstrations "until she was well into her 60s."

Satchel Paige

Satchel Paige. By Lesa Cline-Ransome. Illustrated by James Ransome. Simon and Schuster, 2000. 32 p. Ages 5–10.

LeRoy "Satchel" Paige got his nickname from toting satchels for people at the train station. When he didn't make enough money, he turned to stealing. While in reform school, Satchel got involved with the school's baseball team. He was taught the difference between throwing and pitching. Satchel went on to play semipro ball, where he worked on his specialty pitches: the "hesitation," the "trouble ball," and the "bee ball," a pitch that made the ball go where he wanted it to. Satchel became a big attraction in the Negro league. He would joke to his outfielders, "Why don't you all have a seat. Won't be needing you on this one." White players told him, "We could use you, if only you were white." In 1948, Satchel became the first black pitcher to be drafted in the major leagues. In 1971, Satchel became the first black player to make the National Baseball Hall of Fame.

Also highly recommended: *Satchel Paige: Striking Out Jim Crow.* By James Sturm. Illustrated by Rich Tommaso. Hyperion, 2007. 89 p. Ages 10–14. African American farmer and former ballplayer Emmet Wilson gives an unusual perspective of Satchel Paige in this graphic novel.

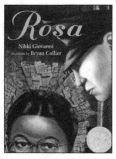

Rosa Parks

Rosa. By Nikki Giovanni. Illustrated by Bryan Collier. Holt, 2005. 40 p. Ages 5–10.

When Rosa Parks refused to give up her bus seat in Montgomery, Alabama, on December 1, 1955, it marked an important day in America's history. Earlier that day, Rosa had a busy day as a seamstress because of the holiday season: "Those elves in the North Pole have nothing on us!" After work, Rosa boarded a city bus to head home. As the vehicle continued to fill up, the bus driver bellowed, "Give me those seats!" Rosa refused.

She was tired of being treated so poorly. She was "tired of 'separate,' and definitely tired of 'not equal.'" After Rosa was arrested, several people worked hard to organize a bus strike. The people were ready to support Rosa's courageous stand. They were proud that their nonviolent movement eventually caused the U.S. Supreme Court to rule that segregation is illegal. Rosa's quiet integrity "turned her no into a YES for change."

Also highly recommended: *Rosa Parks: My Story*. By Rosa Parks. Dial, 1992. 192 p. Ages 10–14. Rosa's autobiography highlights not only her role in the Civil Rights Movement, but also her early childhood.

Gary Paulsen
Guts: The True Stories behind Hatchet *and the Brian Books.* By Gary Paulsen. Delacorte, 2001. 148 p. Ages 10–14.

Gary Paulsen writes about his own wilderness experiences that he used for his fictional character Brian in the book *Hatchet* and its sequels. These include surviving moose attacks, scary plane rides, and eating a strange assortment of food, such as fish eyeballs and animal guts. Gary drew the line at eating raw turtle eggs, though he tried them; they "tasted the way I imagine Vaseline would taste if, somehow, it were rotten." Gary admits there were times he was kind to his fictional character Brian: "He didn't have to face blackflies, which bite and drink blood; horseflies, which bite and take out chunks of flesh; deerflies, which eat meat: wood ticks, which drink blood . . ." Gary surmised that wilderness survival is almost impossible.

Also highly recommended: Gary has written several autobiographies on similar aspects of his life for the same age group. These include: *Caught by the Sea: My Life on Boats,* Delacorte, 2001, 103 p.; *Father Water, Mother Woods: Essays on Fishing and Hunting in the North Woods,* Delacorte, 1994, 159 p.; *My Life in Dog Years,* Delacorte, 1998, 137 p.; *Puppies, Dogs, and Blue Northers: Reflections on Being Raised by a Pack of Sled Dogs,* Harcourt, 1996, 81 p.; and *Woodsong,* Bradbury, 1990, 132 p.

Marie Ahnighito Peary
The Snow Baby: The Arctic Childhood of Admiral E. Peary's Daring Daughter. By Katherine Kirkpatrick. Holiday House, 2007. 50 p. Ages 9–12.

Marie Ahnighito (an Inuit name, ah-nee-GHEE-toe) Peary was born in a tar paper house on the shore of a northern Greenland bay. Her father was the explorer Robert E. Peary, who was attempting to become the first man to reach the North Pole. Peary's wife accompanied him on many expeditions. When the

Inuit people saw the fair-skinned Marie, they called her "Snow Baby" because they thought she was created from snow. When Marie was three years old, she joined her father in his effort to retrieve a thirty-four-ton iron meteorite from Greenland to raise money for his expeditions. Marie was excited when her father handed her a small bottle of wine, held her up, and said, "Now, my little girl, smash your bottle on the meteorite and say, 'I christen thee Ahnighito.'" Another year, while her father was further north, Marie and her mother got stranded on an ice-bound ship for several months. Marie saw it as an adventure. At one point, Marie and her Inuit friends played a successful prank by creating polar bear tracks on the ship's deck, scaring the crew and sending them to hide in their cabins.

Bill Peet

Bill Peet: An Autobiography. By Bill Peet. Houghton Mifflin, 1989. 190 p. Ages 6–12.

As a kid who loved drawing, Bill was disgusted by his art teacher who dictated what the children should draw—"so I drew on the sly in all my other classes." He loved studying animals and credits the desire to learn more about them for turning him into an avid reader. In high school, Bill was failing all of his classes except for gym. "No one failed in physical ed as long as he could do a couple of chin-ups." Another student suggested that Bill take art classes, and his overall grades improved. Bill got a job with Walt Disney and worked on many animated feature films, including *Snow White and the Seven Dwarves, Pinocchio, Dumbo, Alice in Wonderland, Peter Pan, The Sword in the Stone,* and *The Jungle Book.* Bill also started writing and illustrating children's picture books. His first book was *Hubert's Hair-Raising Adventure,* published in 1959. Bill eventually got tired of Disney's mercurial temperament and quit his job at Walt Disney Studios. He felt that his picture book *Chester the Worldly Pig* was autobiographical, with himself represented by Chester, the circus setting as Disney studios, and the master showman Roscoe the Clown representing Walt Disney.

Pelé

Pelé, King of Soccer / Pelé, el rey del fútbol. By Monica Brown. Illustrated by Rudy Gutiérrez. HarperCollins, 2009. 40 p. Ages 4–10.

Biographer Brown uses a bilingual text to profile soccer star Pelé: "Pelé runs across the field like a cheetah, dribbling like a dancer . . . / *Pelé corre por la cancha como un guepardo, regateando como un bailarín . . ."* Pelé grew up in Brazil. His family didn't have enough money for a soccer ball, so they used grapefruits and old socks filled with newspapers. Because Pelé and his friends couldn't afford shoes either, their team became known around town as the "Barefoot Team." Pelé promised his father that someday, Brazil would win the World Cup. At the age of fifteen, Pelé was invited to join a professional team. The coach ordered the skinny Pelé to eat. "For the first time in his life, Pelé had all the food his stomach could hold." At the age of seventeen, he fulfilled his promise to his father and led Brazil to its first World Cup. Pelé went on to lead Brazil to two more World Cups. One of his biggest achievements was to become the first player to reach one thousand goals. "Pelé, O Rei, kicks and scores his thousandth . . . / *Pelé, O Rei, patea y anota su milésimo . . ."*

Pablo Picasso

Just Behave, Pablo Picasso! By Jonah Winter. Illustrated by Kevin Hawkes. Scholastic, 2012. 48 p. Ages 5–10.

Pablo's painting skills as a young man were evident right away. In an art class, surrounded by students older than him, Pablo completed an oil painting while the other students were still working on sketches. He moved from one painting style to another. We see depictions of his artwork as he went through his blue period and then his rose-colored paintings. Pablo was next influenced by African masks: "They seem to have some magical, wonderful power that realistic paintings do not have." The masks inspired him to paint in a new style. Biographer Winter's notes mention this style is known as cubism, an important direction in the history of art. Pablo was hurt by the negative reaction to his new paintings, but he resisted all efforts to go back to realistic paintings. When people said that what he was doing didn't make any sense, Pablo replied, "The chief enemy of Creativity is '*good sense*'!" Today, Pablo Picasso is recognized by many as the first modern artist and "the most original artist of his time."

Bill Pickett

Bill Pickett: Rodeo-Ridin' Cowboy. By Andrea Davis Pinkney. Illustrated by Brian Pinkney. Harcourt, 1996. 32 p. Ages 5–10.

Bill Pickett was the second oldest of the thirteen children born to freed slaves in Texas. He loved watching cowboys on cattle drives go past the family farm.

One day, he noticed a bulldog controlling a cow by holding onto its lower lip. Bill did that very thing when helping two cowhands brand a calf. "Invented there and then by feisty Bill Pickett, that was bulldogging bite-'em style." Bill's reputation grew. He performed at rodeos, earning accolades: "That cowboy's brave clear down to his gizzards!" Bill became known as the Dusky Demon because of the dirt clouds that followed him when he did his tricks. There were some rodeo owners that "believed black cowboys should ride with their own kind." However, in 1905, Bill was hired by Zack Miller to perform with the 101 Ranch Wild West Show, which had "ninety cowboys and cowgirls, three hundred animals, and sixteen acts." The biography ends with Bill's children telling *their* children about their grandfather Bill Pickett, the Dusky Demon.

Horace Pippin

A Splash of Red: The Life and Art of Horace Pippin. By Jen Bryant. Illustrated by Melissa Sweet. Knopf, 2013. 40 p. Ages 5–10.

When Horace was born, his family noted his big hands. "Grandma's hands were big, too—tough, scarred from her slave days in Virginia." After chores, Horace loved to draw pictures on scraps of paper with charcoal. He won a prize for a drawing and received a package containing colored pencils, brushes, and a box of paints. "He painted everyday scenes in natural colors; then he added a splash of red." As an adult, Horace was sent to fight in the war against Germany. He was shot in the shoulder and had limited use of his right arm. One day, he experimented with scorching drawings into wood with a hot iron poker, using his left hand to guide his right. His arm got stronger and he was able draw again. He made several paintings and hung them for sale. Unfortunately, no one bought them. The famous artist N. C. Wyeth saw Horace's work and helped set up an art show. "More than forty years had passed since Horace won his first box of paints. Now, at last, everyone knew he was an artist."

Molly Pitcher

They Called Her Molly Pitcher. By Anne Rockwell. Illustrated by Cynthia von Buhler. Knopf, 2002. 32 p. Ages 6–12.

Mary Hays, nicknamed Molly, followed her husband to George Washington's camp in Valley Forge. She helped cook and clean the bedraggled army. The army was finally ready to fight the British in the spring of 1778 and marched to the colony of New Jersey. Unlike most of the women who stayed behind, Molly followed the army. During the battle, Molly ran back and forth with pitchers of water for the soldiers. The men shouted, "Molly—Pitcher!" Molly's husband was shot, so she took his place loading and firing the cannon.

As Washington rode around the battlefield, he was surprised to see a woman in the middle of the fight. When the skirmish was over, Washington "told her she'd been as brave in battle as any man he'd ever heard of." He gave her the rank of sergeant. The other soldiers knew that Molly earned that distinction. After the war, Molly and her husband, who survived his wounds, went home to Pennsylvania, where she got jobs doing laundry and cleaning houses. "The only fault her employers ever found with her was that she swore like a soldier."

Jackson Pollock

Action Jackson. By Jan Greenberg and Sandra Jordan. Illustrated by Robert Andrew Parker. Roaring Brook, 2002. 32 p. Ages 6–12.

American artist Jackson Pollock was "an athlete with a paintbrush." His studio was in an old barn, and his canvas was on the floor—unlike many artists who put their canvas on the wall or an easel. Jackson wanted "his paintings to be big, big as the sky out West where he grew up, flat as the marshland behind his house." He said, "The painting has a life of its own. I try to let it come through." A reproduction of this painting, titled *Number 1, 1950 (Lavender Mist),* is included as an illustration. The work evoked many reactions from people—shock, anger, confusion, excitement, happiness. There was general agreement, though, that Jackson Pollock was "doing something original, painting in a way that no one has ever seen before." The story line ends with Pollock staring at another canvas, waiting, and then lifting his brush. The back matter includes reactions from critics about his art: "While some reviewers called him the best painter in America, another said his work looked like a plate of baked macaroni." Biographers Greenberg and Jordan honor Pollock for his groundbreaking work by declaring, "A new American art was born."

John Wesley Powell

Down the Colorado: John Wesley Powell, the One-Armed Explorer. By Deborah Kogan Ray. Illustrated by the author. Farrar, Straus and Giroux, 2007. 48 p. Ages 6–12.

Captain John Wesley Powell lost his right arm after a bullet struck him during the Civil War in the Battle of Shiloh. After the war ended, Wes heard about the unmapped region of the Colorado River and decided to plan a scientific expedition. People laughed—"an unknown one-armed geology professor conquering such a vast, dangerous, unexplored territory seemed preposterous." He raised money for four wooden boats and a crew of nine men. Three days into their trip, they encountered a dangerous section they named Disaster Falls.

They lost one boat and a third of their food supply. Will almost lost his life when he was climbing a canyon wall. "Clinging to a rock face with his one good arm, he was saved by George Bradley, who took off his pants and used them to pull Wes up to safety." The rough conditions of the Colorado River changed the status of the expedition from research to "survival as the only goal." They made it to safety, and Wes went on to become a national hero.

Juan Quezada
The Pot That Juan Built. By Nancy Andrews-Goebel. Illustrated by David Diaz. Lee & Low Books, 2002. 32 p. Ages 5–10.

Juan became very interested in the pottery-making process of the Casa Grandes people, who lived in his region of Mexico hundreds of years before. He became a professional potter, trained others in his village, and transformed the village of Mata Ortiz from an impoverished one "into a prosperous community of working artists." Each verso (left-sided) page builds a cumulative poem in the style of the nursery rhyme "The House That Jack Built." The opposite page contains information about Juan. One page reads, "These are the ants that led the way / And showed Juan a vein of special clay." The following page describes how Juan happened across a colony of ants while he was searching for minerals and clay. The ants were carrying bits of a special white clay that Juan was able to use for his pottery. The entire poem is built up to nineteen lines and reads down to the last, "The beautiful pot that Juan built." In 1999, Juan was presented with the National Arts and Science Award, "the highest honor for any artist in Mexico."

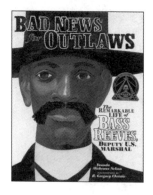

Bass Reeves
Bad News for Outlaws: The Remarkable Life of Bass Reeves, Deputy U.S. Marshal. By Vaunda Micheaux Nelson. Illustrated by R. Gregory Christie. Carolrhoda, 2009. 40 p. Ages 8–12.

Bass Reeves was a young slave in Texas who became a proficient marksman. One sharpshooter stated, "He could shoot the left hind leg off a contented fly sitting on a mule's ear at a hundred yards and never ruffle a hair." After the Civil War, Bass was hired as a deputy marshal to help track criminals. One time, Bass was after two outlaw brothers who were hiding at their mother's cabin. In disguise, Bass showed up and claimed a posse was after him. He spent the night with the brothers. They were surprised to wake up in handcuffs. "Their ma was fit to be tied. As Bass led her sons away, she followed for three miles, calling him every bad name she knew." Another time, Bass rode into a large angry mob gathered for a lynching; "this was near as risky as a grasshopper landing on an anthill." The crowd recognized Bass and dared not interfere as he cut the man down and rode away with him. It was said that he "was the most feared deputy U.S. marshal that was ever heard of."

Lily Renée

Lily Renée, Escape Artist: From Holocaust Survivor to Comic Book Pioneer. By Trina Robbins. Illustrated by Anne Timmons and Mo Oh. Graphic Universe, 2011. 96 p. Ages 9–14.

When the Nazis invaded Austria, Lily participated in the *Kindertransport* operation that evacuated ten thousand children to England. When Lily moved in with her English host family, she soon learned that the household mother was mean. Lily often went hungry, so she ran away. She found work at a maternity hospital and helped take the babies to the shelter when the Nazis bombed Leeds. She constantly worried about her parents, who were left behind; she eventually rejoined them in America. There Lily found work in New York City as a model. She also drew catalogue pictures for fifty cents an hour. Lily's break came when she got a job working for a comic book publisher. One of the series she drew was about a female pilot who fought the Nazis. She started getting fan mail addressed to Mr. Renée. "I sign my work 'L. Renée.' They can't imagine that I could be a woman." Her grandchildren, many years later, were proud that "grandmother was a comic book artist." It's appropriate that her biography is done in a graphic novel format.

Margaret and H. A. Rey

The Journey That Saved Curious George: The True Wartime Escape of Margaret and H. A. Rey. By Louise Borden. Illustrated by Allan Drummond. Houghton Mifflin, 2005. 80 p. Ages 7–12.

Hans Augusto Reyersbach and Margarete Waldstein both grew up in Germany. The two artists got married and shortened their name to Rey: "It was a name to remember." They moved to Paris and began writing stories for children. One of their characters was a curious monkey named Fifi. In 1940, the German army advanced on Paris. There were no cars or trains for the Reys to leave the city, so Hans bought one bicycle and parts for another. "H. A. Rey, the artist, became a bicycle maker." Among their possessions were manuscripts, including *The Adventures of Fifi*. "More than five million people were on the roads of France that day" as people fled the German army. At one point, an important official suspected them of being spies, until he "thumbed through the pages of *The Adventures of Fifi*. 'Ah . . . un livre pour les enfants.'" The monkey had saved the Reys. They made it to America, where their first book was finally published. "French monkey Fifi would change his name, and it would become one to remember . . . the well-loved Curious George."

Diego Rivera
Diego Rivera: An Artist for the People. By Susan Goldman Rubin. Abrams, 2013. 56 p. Ages 10–14.

Painter Diego Rivera was restless after studying art in Paris: "The secret of my best work is that it is Mexican." He decided to tackle mural painting. Diego began drawing as a young child. He drew an accurate, yet unflattering sketch of his mother. She tore it up. When he was older, Diego was six feet tall and over three hundred pounds. He attracted a lot of attention from women, despite his size and poor bathing habits. One woman was artist Frida Kahlo. She affectionately called him Frog-Face, and he told her that she had the face of a dog. Diego created immense and sometimes controversial murals in both Mexico and the United States. One of his murals in New York City was destroyed because he added a depiction of Communist Russian leader Vladimir Lenin. Diego is perhaps best known for showing all aspects of Mexican history, including the struggles of the working class. "For the first time, Indians and *campesinos,* people from the countryside, saw themselves as contributing to the culture of their country." Near the end of his life in the 1950s, Diego stated that the "most joyous moments of my life were those I had spent in painting."

Jackie Robinson and Pee Wee Reese
Teammates. By Peter Golenbock. Illustrated by Paul Bacon. Harcourt, 1990. 32 p. Ages 5–10.

Branch Rickey, the general manager of the Brooklyn Dodgers, thought segregation in America was unfair. He wanted to recruit excellent ballplayers, regardless of their skin color. Rickey felt he found that man in Jackie Robinson, who became the first African American to play for a Major League Baseball team. Many teammates avoided Jackie; opposing players called him names and tried to injure him. He often felt alone. He couldn't even stay in the same hotels as his white teammates. However, Pee Wee Reese refused to sign a petition circulated among Dodger players to throw Jackie off the team. At a game in Cincinnati, the fans were yelling hateful things at Jackie, who was playing first base. "Pee Wee decided to take a stand." He walked over to first base and looked into Jackie's eyes. "The first baseman had done nothing wrong to provoke the hostility except that he sought to be treated as an equal." Pee Wee put his arm around Jackie's shoulder, which caused a gasp from the crowd. Pee Wee's actions told the world, "I am standing by him. This man is my teammate."

Alice Roosevelt

What to Do About Alice? How Alice Roosevelt Broke the Rules, Charmed the World, and Drove Her Father Teddy Crazy! By Barbara Kerley. Illustrated by Edwin Fotheringham. Scholastic, 2008. 48 p. Ages 5–10.

Theodore Roosevelt accomplished many great things in his life: he herded cattle in the Badlands, led a charge up Kettle Hill, and was a successful politician. But he had a problem—his daughter Alice. She was an adventurous, spunky girl who was constantly on the go, looking for new adventures. "Father called it 'Running Riot.' Alice called it 'eating up the world.'" She didn't even let a short period of wearing leg braces slow her down. She was nineteen years old when her father was elected president and the family moved into the White House. Alice brought her pet snake Emily Spinach with her. Roosevelt said to a friend, "I can be president of the United State, or I can control Alice. I cannot possibly DO BOTH." Her father also warned her to be on "her BEST OFFICIAL BEHAVIOR" and not talk to reporters. It didn't work. Even after Alice got married, she filled her life to the fullest. The book concludes "that Theodore Roosevelt never quite solved . . . What to do about Alice?"

Eleanor Roosevelt

Eleanor Roosevelt: A Life of Discovery. By Russell Freedman. Clarion, 1993. 198 p. Ages 10–14.

Eleanor was a timid child who was "afraid of almost everything." When her mother called her "Granny," Eleanor felt that she "wanted to sink through the floor in shame." As a teen, she attended school outside of London and blossomed. Her favorite teacher "had a special sympathy for unpopular causes. She always championed the underdogs." Eleanor's strong personality began to emerge. She went on to marry her distant cousin Franklin and became a young mother. The couple had an active social schedule and "any shyness was wearing off rapidly." When Franklin lost the use of his legs to polio, Eleanor refused to treat him like an invalid. Eleanor broke the traditional role of First Lady when Franklin became president. She was an active crusader of many causes and visited a lot of people who were down and out because of the Great Depression. "Her sympathetic visits created a feeling among millions of Americans that someone in the highest levels of government cared about their problems."

Also highly recommended: *Eleanor, Quiet No More.* By Doreen Rappaport. Illustrated by Gary Kelley. Hyperion, 2009. 48 p. Ages 8–10. This picture book biography includes several quotes by Eleanor Roosevelt.

Theodore Roosevelt
Teedie: The Story of Young Teddy Roosevelt. By Don Brown. Illustrated by the author. Houghton Mifflin, 2009. 32 p. Ages 5–10.

Teedie was a delicate boy and small for his age. He had poor eyesight and weak muscles, and he suffered from asthma. To cure his affliction, his parents experimented with cures, having him gulp coffee or puff a cigar. Despite his physical condition, Teedie had a strong mind. He was very curious about the world. He exercised faithfully and even took up boxing lessons after being confronted by bullies on a trip. Teedie became Teddy. After graduating from college, he became a cowboy in the Dakota Badlands. "When a gun-toting cowboy made fun of Teddy's eyeglasses, he flattened the cowboy with one punch." He returned to New York and achieved many things: New York City police commissioner, assistant secretary of the navy, colonel in the war between America and Spain (with his cavalry known as the Rough Riders), governor of New York, and, at the age of forty-two, the youngest president of the United States. The final illustration in the book shows Roosevelt surrounded with curved text listing many of his accomplishments. The biography ends with the statement, "The undersize boy had become a larger-than-life man."

Wilma Rudolph
Wilma Unlimited: How Wilma Rudolph Became the World's Fastest Woman. By Kathleen Krull. Illustrated by David Diaz. Harcourt, 1996. 44 p. Ages 5–10.

Wilma was born into a Clarksville, Tennessee, family with nineteen older siblings. She was a small, sickly child. Wilma contracted polio and had to ride the bus fifty miles away twice a week to the "nearest hospital that would treat black patients." She wore metal leg braces, and the kids at school made fun of her. She worked hard with her leg exercises even though they hurt. One dramatic day, Wilma took her braces off and walked down the church aisle during service. Wilma became an athlete, helping her high school basketball team go to the state tournament. A college coach spotted her and helped her get a track-and-field scholarship to Tennessee State University. She was the first in her family to attend college. Wilma participated in the 1960 Olympic Games as a runner and won her first gold medal in the 100-meter dash despite a twisted ankle. She won a second gold medal for the 200-meter dash. After she burst across the finish line for her third gold medal, "Wilma Rudolph, once known as the sickliest child in Clarksville, had become the fastest woman in the world."

Babe Ruth
Becoming Babe Ruth. By Matt Tavares. Illustrated by the author. Candlewick, 2003. 40 p. Ages 4–10.

Babe Ruth is recognized by many as one of baseball's greatest players. George Herman Ruth Jr. often got into trouble. In 1902, when he was seven, George was sent to Saint Mary's. It wasn't a prison, "but the eight hundred boys who live there call themselves inmates." George excelled at baseball under the tutelage of Brother Matthias. He even played in the band. When George was sixteen, he was the biggest, strongest boy at Saint Mary's, as well as the best ballplayer. In the minor leagues, he earned his nickname "Babe" because of his young age. Babe moved up to the major leagues and quickly became a star pitcher. The Boston Red Sox switched him to outfield so that he could bat every day. The nation was shocked when Babe was traded to the New York Yankees. When a fire destroyed Saint Mary's, Babe helped out. The school band was invited to travel with the Yankees, guests of Babe. "They play a concert in the stands before each game and another concert every night." The book ends with Babe visiting the school years after it was rebuilt.

Sacagawea
Sacagawea. By Lise Erdrich. Illustrated by Julie Buffalohead. Carolrhoda, 2003. 40 p. Ages 6–12.

A young Shoshone girl living in a Rocky Mountain valley was kidnapped by Hidatsa warriors. They took the girl east to the Great Plains. That girl was named Sacagawea, a name that meant "Bird Woman." She was later given in marriage to French Canadian fur trapper Toussaint Charbonneau, a man twenty years her age. Charbonneau convinced explorers Meriwether Lewis and William Clark to hire him as a guide and interpreter. Sacagawea and her newborn child joined the expedition. Sacagawea became a more valuable member of the Corps of Discovery than her husband. She knew which plants kept the men healthy. When they encountered the Shoshone, Sacagawea was reunited with her family and acted as a translator. She stayed with the explorers all the way to the ocean. On the return trip, the expedition split in two. Sacagawea joined Clark on his route along the Yellowstone River. The parties reunited near the Knife River lodges. Sacagawea's part of this journey was over. The author's notes point out that there is disagreement on the pronunciation of Sacagawea's name: "There is no soft g sound in the Hidatsa language, so the name would have sounded more like sa-KA-ga-WEE-ah than SA-ka-ja-WEE-ah."

Alberto Santos-Dumont

The Fabulous Flying Machines of Alberto Santos-Dumont. By Victoria Griffith. Illustrated by Eva Montanari. Abrams, 2011. 32 p. Ages 5–10.

A few years after the Wright Brothers glided in the air over Kitty Hawk, Brazilian born Albert Santos-Dumont, dubbed the "Father of Flight," flew the first self-propelled airplane over a field outside of Paris, France. In 1903, Albert often flew a dirigible over the city. "The doorman of the hat shop, used to Albert's unusual choice of transportation, rushed forward to take the rope and tie it to a post." Albert frequented the hat store because the hydrogen gas he used for his airship often caught on fire; "Albert often used hats to quench the flames." In 1906, in a field outside of Paris, Albert was readying his new flying machine. A competitor named Louis Blériot showed up at the same time with his own flying machine. Albert graciously let Louis go first. Louis failed after three attempts. Albert's plane flew on its own power for twenty-one seconds. Albert hoped that his invention would bring world peace. His friend Louis Cartier "wasn't sure, but he knew the airplane would change the world forever."

Tony Sarg

Balloons over Broadway: The True Story of the Puppeteer of Macy's Parade. By Melissa Sweet. Illustrated by the author. Houghton Mifflin, 2011. 40 p. Ages 5–10.

When young Tony Sarg was growing up on the farm, he rigged a pulley system so he could feed the chickens from his bed: "Tony stayed snug in his bed, and his dad, so impressed, never made Tony do another chore." As an adult, Tony

rom the time he was a little boy, Tony Sarg loved to figure out how to make things move. He once said he became a marionette man when he was only six years old.

Figure 1.6. From ***Balloons over Broadway: The True Story of the Puppeteer of Macy's Parade*** by Melissa Sweet, illustrated by the author.

became known for the marionettes he made. Macy's, billed as the biggest store on earth, asked Tony to make a puppet parade for their window displays. When Macy's sponsored their first parade, it was a success thanks in part to Tony's floats. For the next parade, he was asked to make something even more spectacular. Tony created large creatures inspired by rod puppets, "some as high as sixteen feet, [which] spilled into the streets, and the crowds cheered wildly." As the crowds grew each year, Tony realized his puppets needed to be higher off the ground just to be seen. He thought, "What if the controls were below and the puppet could rise up?" He ordered balloons made of rubberized silk filled with helium. The big test happened that dark Thanksgiving morning in 1928. "It was a parade New Yorkers would never forget!"

Allen Say

Drawing from Memory. By Allen Say. Illustrated by the author. Scholastic, 2011. 64 p. Ages 10–14.

Caldecott Award–winning artist Allen Say describes his life growing up in Japan in a format similar to graphic novels. Allen wanted to become a cartoonist. His father told him that artists were "not respectable." Allen had a first-grade teacher who told him that he had talent; "no one had told me that before." At the age of twelve, Allen was stunned to learn that he was given his own apartment to live in. He read an account of a boy named Tokida, who ran away from home and walked 350 miles to work as a cartoonist for a newspaper. Noro Shinpei, a famous cartoonist, took in Tokida as an apprentice. This story inspired Allen to approach Shinpei himself. Thus began Allen's long friendship with Master Noro, referred to as Sensei. In time, Allen had a chance to go to America. Sensei told Allen, "Traveling is the greatest teacher of all." Before Allen left Japan, he burned his sketchbooks and left his apartment empty like he found it three years earlier: "I was ready to start a new life with what I could carry on my back."

Charles Schulz

Sparky: The Life and Art of Charles Schulz. By Beverly Gherman. Chronicle, 2010. 125 p. Ages 8–14.

Charles was nicknamed "Sparky" as a baby. Comics were a big influence in his life. One teacher told him, "Someday, Charles, you're going to be an artist." Charles was influenced by his family and surroundings. His father was a barber, same as the father of his famous cartoon creation Charlie Brown. Lucy was modeled after his stepdaughter Meredith. Charles's son Monty was the inspiration behind Linus. When Charles's mother was dying, she told him to name their next dog Snoopy. Charlie Brown himself was created after Charles had his heart broken by a red-haired woman, the inspiration for the red-haired girl in the comic strip. When Charles realized good guys don't always win, "Charlie Brown's personality was born at that moment." Charles's first published piece was a drawing of his dog for *Ripley's Believe It or Not* with the caption "A hunting dog that eats pins, tacks and razor blades is owned by C. F. Schulz, St. Paul,

Minn." Many of the *Peanuts* strips scattered throughout the biography relate in some way to Charles's real life. He lived to the age of seventy-seven, and at that time, over 2,600 newspapers carried *Peanuts.*

Jon Scieszka
Knucklehead: Tall Tales & Mostly True Stories about Growing Up Scieszka. By Jon Scieszka. Viking, 2008. 106 p. Ages 8–12.

Popular children's humor author Jon Scieszka (SHEH-ska) remembers the first time he heard the name *Knucklehead.* His father, who found that his toast tasted funny, asked, "What Knucklehead put an army man in the toaster?" Scieszka shares several stories about growing up in a house of six active boys. Jon and his older brother Jim charged their friends ten cents to watch the youngest brother, Jeff, chew cigarette butts. The boys put a Boy Scout hat on their second youngest brother, Brian, for Halloween and took him treat-or-treating as the Smallest Boy Scout in the World. They tied up their babysitter for two hours in a closet. And there was that incident when their cat threw up in the car on a trip that led to a chain-reaction "group-puke horror." Jon once made the mistake of answering with a joke when teacher Sister Margaret Mary asked, "What's so funny, Mr. Scieszka?" The author feels his fellow students' hysterical reaction "set me on my lifelong path of answering that classic question, 'What's so funny, Mr. Scieszka?'"

Irena Sendler
Irena's Jars of Secrets. By Marcia Vaughan. Illustrated by Ron Mazellan. Lee & Low Books, 2011. 40 p. Ages 9–12.

Irena's father told her that if she ever saw someone drowning, she must jump in and try to save the person, even if she could not swim herself. When Hitler invaded Poland during World War II, Irena remembered her father's words and tried to help the Jewish people, who were "drowning" in her mind and heart. Irena joined a secret organization called Zegota that smuggled children out of the ghetto. During one tense episode, Irena, dressed as a nurse, and a driver were smuggling a baby in an ambulance. A guard started to search the vehicle, so Irena hit the dog that they kept in the ambulance. When the dog barked, the soldier got impatient and waved them through the gate. Irena kept a secret list of the children's real names and their new secret identities so that the families could one day be reunited. She buried the lists in jars in a friend's garden. After the war, Irena recovered the jars and helped find living relatives for some of the children.

Dr. Seuss
The Boy on Fairfield Street: How Ted Geisel Grew Up to Become Dr. Seuss. By Kathleen Krull. Illustrated by Steve Johnson and Lou Fancher. Random House, 2004. 48 p. Ages 5–10.

"Once upon a time, there lived a boy who feasted on books and was wild about animals." Ted Geisel enjoyed his boyhood neighborhood in Springfield, Massachusetts. After all, it was "exactly three blocks from the public library. And it was just six blocks from the zoo." Ted had some friends who joined him in ear-wiggling contests. Unfortunately, Ted was teased by other kids for being of German descent at a time when many Americans were upset about events in Europe. That wasn't the only obstacle he overcame. A high school art teacher warned him that he would never be successful in art. Ted was voted "least likely to succeed" by college mates. When Ted's cartoons started selling, he changed his name to "Dr. Seuss." Seuss was his mother's maiden name as well as his middle name, and the addition of "doctor" tickled him and added that "ring to it that he and his family liked so much." The book ends with Ted moving to New York City. "He was twenty-two years old, and his future looked bright."

Anna Howard Shaw
A Voice from the Wilderness: The Story of Anna Howard Shaw. By Don Brown. Illustrated by the author. Houghton Mifflin, 2001. 32 p. Ages 5–10.

Anna, her mother, and her siblings crossed the Atlantic Ocean in 1851 to join their father in America. Shortly after they left England, a storm damaged their ship and they had to return. Anna's father thought they had perished and was overjoyed when they eventually arrived. The family settled in Massachusetts, where Anna ate a banana for the first time. She cried because she hadn't known the peels weren't supposed to be eaten. They turned into pioneers, traveling to Michigan to establish a farm deep in the woods. "The cabin stood one hundred miles from the railroad, forty miles from a post office, and six miles from the nearest neighbor." Since there was no school in the area, Anna "read the old newspapers that were hung in the cabin as wallpaper." Anna had a desire to communicate with people. She would stand on stumps and talk to the trees. She eventually went off to college and spoke out for the right for women to vote. "The little girl who had once preached to the hushed forest now spoke to audiences around the world."

Paula Young Shelton

Child of the Civil Rights Movement. By Paula Young Shelton. Illustrated by Raúl Colón. Schwartz & Wade Books, 2010. 40 p. Ages 5–10.

Paula, the daughter of activist Andrew Young, grew up in the middle of the civil rights movement of the 1960s. Jim Crow laws were everywhere. These were laws that forbade African Americans from voting and forced them to sit in the back of the bus and in movie theater balconies. As a very young girl, Paula imagined an actual big black crow squawking, "CAWWW, CAWWW, you can't sit there!" Her parents took the family to eat at a new restaurant and were refused service. Paula threw a tantrum: "I screamed at the top of my lungs, my very first protest, my own little sit-in." Her father was a close friend of Martin Luther King Jr., whom Paula called Uncle Martin. Several families would get together and plan protest marches. Paula and her sisters marched with thousands at Selma. "It would take four days to march the fifty miles from Selma to Montgomery, the National Guard escorting peaceful protesters the whole way to keep them safe." Shortly afterwards, President Johnson signed "the bill that would make sure *all* people—black and white—could vote and no one could stop them."

Robert Smalls

Seven Miles to Freedom: The Robert Smalls Story. By Janet Halfmann. Illustrated by Duane Smith. Lee & Low Books, 2008. 40 p. Ages 7–12.

Robert was a slave in South Carolina who learned to pilot boats. When Robert had a baby girl named Elizabeth, he and his wife, Hannah, were "saddened by the realization that Elizabeth did not belong to them. She was the property of Hannah's master." Robert planned to buy his wife and daughter's freedom, but before he could do that, the Civil War started. "For slaves such as Robert and Hannah war brought uncertainty, but also hope." Robert made a plan to steal his captain's boat and head for Union lines, just seven miles away. Robert and his companions loaded Confederate cannons and made off with the ship. They met a rowboat carrying family members of the crew. "Wearing the captain's hat and responding with the secret steam whistle signals," Robert slipped past three Confederate forts and delivered the boat to the Union navy. The afterword mentions that Robert was elected to U.S. Congress in 1875. In 2004, the U.S. Army christened the first army vessel ever named for an African American—the *Major General Robert Smalls.*

Elizabeth Cady Stanton

Elizabeth Leads the Way: Elizabeth Cady Stanton and the Right to Vote. By Tanya Lee Stone. Illustrated by Rebecca Gibbon. Holt, 2008. 32 p. Ages 5–10.

Elizabeth was shocked when her father, a judge, told her about a case where a woman lost her farm after her husband died. According to the law, "*nothing* belonged to her.*" Elizabeth chafed at the notion that only men could change laws because only men could vote. Elizabeth fought for women's right to vote. "This idea was so shocking, so huge, so daring—Elizabeth's friends gasped out loud!" Her battle cry became "Have it, we must. Use it, we will." On July 19, 1848, Elizabeth read aloud a Declaration of Rights and Sentiments that challenged the idea that "all *men* are created equal." Arguments broke out, and news of the meeting went from coast to coast. "Many said Elizabeth must be stopped. But she was unstoppable. She changed America forever." The author's note mentions that Elizabeth lived until an old age. Even though the Nineteenth Amendment, giving women the right to vote, was passed eighteen years after her death, "it was Elizabeth who had gotten the ball rolling."

Toni Stone

Catching the Moon: The Story of a Young Girl's Baseball Dream. By Crystal Hubbard. Illustrated by Randy DuBurke. Lee & Low Books, 2005. 32 p. Ages 5–10.

Young Marcenia Lyle loved to play baseball with the boys. She wanted to grow up to be a professional baseball player, even though her Papa said, "She'll be what every other girl in this neighborhood will be . . . A teacher, a nurse . . ." Mr. Street, who ran a summer baseball camp, watched the kids play one day. Marcenia scored three runs and hit a home run, but Mr. Street told her that girls weren't allowed at his camp. Mr. Street changed his mind after watching Marcenia steal home. She finally got her father's approval to play and realized her dream was coming true. Marcenia changed her name to Toni Stone and played for semiprofessional and minor league Negro teams. When she was thirty-two years old, she filled a spot that Hank Aaron vacated and became the first female member of an all-male professional baseball team.

Also highly recommended: *A Strong Right Arm: The Story of Mamie "Peanut" Johnson.* By Michelle Y. Green. Dial, 2002. 111 p. Ages 10–14. Mamie Johnson was a teammate of Toni Stone and one of only three women to ever play in the Negro Leagues.

Igor Stravinsky and Vaslav Nijinsky

When Stravinsky Met Nijinsky: Two Artists, Their Ballet, and One Extraordinary Riot. By Lauren Stringer. Illustrated by the author. Harcourt, 2013. 32 p. Ages 6–12.

Composer Igor Stravinsky and choreographer Vaslav Nijinsky collaborated to create the celebrated—and controversial—ballet *The Rite of Spring.* They inspired each other. Stravinsky's music changed and "his piano pirouetted a puppet, his tuba leaped a loping bear." Nijinsky's "arms and legs sang from strings, and his feet began to pom-di-di-pom like timpani." Together, they worked to create a piece of art inspired by their old home, Russia. Some of the dancers and musicians were so disenchanted with this unusual new work, they walked out of practice. At the premiere of the show, some audience members started booing, throwing items, and stamping their feet. Other audience members loved what they heard and saw. They cheered and threw items and stamped their feet. Igor and Vaslav concluded afterward that "something very different and new began that remarkable night." The author's notes mention that a riot erupted during this performance and police had to be called in. No matter what side the audience members were on, they had all witnessed "the birth of modern music and modern dance" on that day in 1913.

Chiune Sugihara

Passage to Freedom: The Sugihara Story. By Ken Mochizuki. Illustrated by Dom Lee. Lee & Low Books, 1997. 32 p. Ages 6–12.

Chiune Sugihara was a Japanese diplomat stationed in Lithuania in 1940. His story is told through the eyes of his five-year-old son, Hiroki. Hundreds of people gathered outside of Chiune's office, crowded against the gate. Representatives of the group—Polish Jews fleeing the Nazis—pleaded with Chiune to grant them visas, "official written permission to travel through another country." They wanted Chiune to allow them to cross the Soviet Union into Japan, where they could travel to safety in other countries. When Chiune asked the Japanese government for permission, they refused. He asked again. They refused once more. With the support of his family, Chiune decided to take action. "I may have to disobey my government, but if I don't, I will be disobeying God." For days, Chiune handwrote hundreds of visas. When the German soldiers arrived in Lithuania, they ordered Chiune and his family to leave. Even as his train pulled out of the station, he wrote and threw out more visas. Hiroki states that he didn't realize the significance of what his father did back then. "I do now."

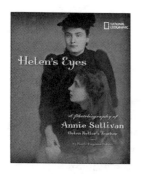

Annie Sullivan

Helen's Eyes: A Photobiography of Annie Sullivan, Helen Keller's Teacher. By Marfé Ferguson Delano. National Geographic, 2008. 64 p. Ages 8–14.

Annie Sullivan was known as "the miracle worker" through her close association with Helen Keller. Annie herself had a rough childhood. She started losing her eyesight at the age of five. Annie and her brother, Jimmie, were sent to a poorhouse. After Jimmie died, Annie lamented, "I believe very few children have ever been so completely left alone as I was." At the age of twenty, she answered a position to care for a six-year-old "little deaf-mute and blind" girl. Annie and young Helen Keller struggled against each other. At one point, Helen knocked out two of Annie's teeth. Annie said, "I never saw such strength and endurance in a child. But fortunately for both of us, I am a little stronger and quite as obstinate when I set out." The two became inseparable the rest of their lives. When Annie passed away, Helen was there holding "the hand that had spelled the world to Helen for nearly half a century."

Also highly recommended: *Helen's Big World: The Life of Helen Keller.* By Doreen Rappaport. Illustrated by Matt Tavares. Hyperion, 2012. 40 p. Ages 5–9. This picture book biography covers Helen's complete life.

Hiromi Suzuki

Hiromi's Hands. By Lynne Barasch. Illustrated by the author. Lee & Low Books, 2007. 40 p. Ages 5–10.

Hiromi became one of the first female sushi chefs in New York. Her grandmother encouraged her father to become a sushi chef in Tokyo, Japan. "Papa's mother was glad he was a boy. A girl could never be a sushi chef." Years later, when Hiromi's father moved to New York, he met his wife, and Hiromi was born. When Hiromi was eight years old, she convinced her father to take her to the fish market, where he taught her about the different types of fish: "I laughed when he showed me how fluke was different from the other fish. Fluke had both eyes on the same side of its head!" Hiromi loved being with her father in this grown-up world. She began her own apprenticeship under him. Hiromi worked hard to become a professional sushi chef, an *itamae-san*. At last, the owner of the Kamehachi restaurant in Tokyo came by and ate one of Hiromi's culinary creations. He congratulated her and said, "You are truly *itamae-san.*" A helpful glossary and pronunciation guide is included.

Bob and Joe Switzer

The Day-Glo Brothers: The True Story of Bob and Joe Switzer's Bright Ideas and Brand-New Colors. By Chris Barton. Illustrated by Tony Persiani. Charlesbridge, 2009. 44 p. Ages 6–12.

Bob Switzer had seizures and double vision and had to lie in bed in a dark basement. His brother Joe practiced magic acts. Joe thought that a glowing substance, known as fluorescence, could jazz up his act. He experimented in the basement, and Bob was eager to help. One night, they noticed that "the chemical-stained label on a bottle of eyewash emitted a yellow glow." They learned how to mix chemicals to make glow-in-the-dark paints. While the Switzer brothers became successful selling their paint for various purposes, they were eager to make a paint that would glow even in sunlight. They finally made the right combination of fluorescent orange and hot alcohol and soaked a billboard's fabric panels with it. The billboard appeared as if it were on fire. They had invented a new color and called it Fire Orange. They made other glowing colors. At this time, World War II had begun, and the military purchased these new Day-Glo paints for signals. "After the war Bob and Joe's colors made them rich. Day-Glo began to brighten everyday life back home."

Maria Tallchief

Tallchief: America's Prima Ballerina. By Maria Tallchief and Rosemary Wells. Illustrated by Gary Kelley. Viking, 1999. 32 p. Ages 6–12.

Maria Tallchief was born on the Osage Indian Reservation in Oklahoma. Her father was a full-blooded Osage; her mother was a Scotch-Irish woman. Maria's family had some money because they owned the oil rights on their land. She took piano and dance lessons. "The secret of music is that it is something like a house with many rooms. The frame of good music has to be strong enough to hold the weight of a whole symphony, and delicate enough to break the heart." Maria lived during a time and location when dancing and other native ceremonies were forbidden by white society. Her family eventually moved to Los Angeles, where she had to choose between piano and dancing. Her new dancing teacher, Madame Nijinski—sister of the great Nijinksi—told her, "When you sleep, you must sleep like a dancer. When you stand and wait for the bus, you must wait for the bus like a dancer." The book ends with seventeen-year-old Maria heading on a train to see about joining the Ballets Russes de Monte Carlo in New York City.

Figure 1.7. From ***Piano Starts Here: The Young
Art Tatum*** by Robert Andrew Parker.

Art Tatum

Piano Starts Here: The Young Art Tatum. By Robert Andrew Parker. Schwartz &
Wade Books, 2008. 40 p. Ages 5–10.

A piano sat quietly in Art Tatum's Toledo house until the day he could "reach
the keyboard on tiptoe." Art started losing his sight at an early age, but his
hands got to know the keys. When Art's mother called him to supper, Art

would say, "I'll be right back. Piano, don't go away." He started to play the piano for church at the age of ten. Invitations to play at other places soon followed. Art played the player piano at a nearby café. The owner asked him, "Arthur, was that you or the piano? I know that it was you—the player piano isn't that fast!" With the money Art started making, he bought his mother a music box and his father a baseball mitt. Bandleaders invited Art to play for them, taking him away from home. Art states that even after he became famous, "late at night, as people sway around me and my foot is tapping, I think of our home in Toledo."

Annie Edson Taylor

Queen of the Falls. By Chris Van Allsburg. Illustrated by the author. Houghton Mifflin, 2010. 40 p. Ages 5–10.

Annie Edson Taylor was the first person to successfully ride in a barrel down Niagara Falls, a drop "from a height that is as tall as a seventeen-story build-ing." She did it at the age of sixty-two. A few years before she accomplished this feat, Annie worried about money. She decided to go over Niagara Falls in a barrel, become famous, and speak to audiences who would surely want to hear of her exploits. The day finally came. Inside the barrel, Annie felt "com-plete discombobulation. As she shot through the rapids that led to the falls, she was upside down one second, on her side the next, then on her back." Over the falls she went. When her barrel was retrieved and opened, there was Annie, dizzy, bruised, and sore with a cut on her forehead, but otherwise healthy. Unfortunately, the crowds never materialized to hear her story, and her man-ager ran off with her famous barrel. On the tenth anniversary of her ride, Annie told a reporter that she didn't become rich for her feat. But she was content to say, "I was the one who did it."

Raina Telgemeier

Smile. By Raina Telgemeier. Illustrated by the author. Graphix, 2010. 218 p. Ages 10–14.

In this autobiographical graphic novel, Raina shares how she not only dealt with normal adolescent worries, but she also underwent major dental issues. At the age of twelve, Raina fell and lost her front teeth. The dentist worked hard to restore them. When Raina woke up the next day, she asked "What'th thith thtuff on my teeth??" That stuff was a sort of cast. Unfortunately, when the cast came off,

Raina's front teeth were higher up than her other teeth. She thought she looked like a vampire. She then had to wear braces. Raina moved up to seventh grade the following year and became interested in a particular boy. Her friends, who had constantly teased her about her teeth, made fun of her crush. "Raina likes a tiny-tot sixth grader!!" Raina next had to get her front teeth pulled to allow the braces to pull her other teeth together. She lamented that the teen years were no fun. In high school, Raina ditched her mean friends, made new friends, received attention for her drawing skills, and finally, after four and a half years of treatment, got rid of her braces.

Jim Thorpe

Jim Thorpe: Original All-American. By Joseph Bruchac. Dial, 2006. 273 p. Ages 10–14.

When Jim was born, his mother called him "Wathohuck . . . Bright Path." Years later, a teacher called him "Stupid." Jim hated school as a boy and kept running away. Jim was sent to the Carlisle Indian Industrial School in Carlisle, Pennsylvania, miles from his home in Oklahoma. His father told him, "Son, you are an Indian. I want you to show other races what an Indian can do." Jim found sports and became a successful athlete in baseball, football, and track. Jim first caught the eye of legendary coach Pop Warner when he cleared a height at the high jump that the varsity boys couldn't make. Jim further impressed Warner during football practice when he ran over several tacklers, leaving them on the ground "spread out like a forest of trees knocked over by a tornado." Biographer Bruchac details the rest of Thorpe's life, including his triumphs and subsequent controversies at the 1912 Olympic Games.

Also highly recommended: *Jim Thorpe's Bright Path.* By Joseph Bruchac. Illustrated by S. D. Nelson. Lee & Low Books, 2008. 40 p. Ages 5–10. This picture book account of Thorpe follows his pre-Carlisle school days as a young boy.

Leon Tillage

Leon's Story. By Leon Tillage. Farrar, Straus and Giroux, 1997. 107 p. Ages 10–14.

Leon grew up in North Carolina, the son of black sharecroppers. A school bus carrying white students would sometimes stop so that they could throw rocks at the black kids. "The larger black kids would act like decoys. They would keep the little children from getting hit." Leon surmises the white parents told their children that blacks had no soul or feelings. "You could hit them or whatever, and you wouldn't hurt them." The most horrific event in Leon's life happened on his fifteenth birthday. A carload of white boys struck Leon's parents with their vehicle, killing Leon's father and injuring his mother. The next day, the teenage driver and his father showed up at Leon's home. The father reluctantly gave Leon's mother one hundred dollars and ordered his son to apologize. The son refused. The father apologized for his son and said that these things happen. Leon went on to participate in many civil rights marches. "What we cared about was who are you to tell us what we can and can't do in America, the land of freedom, the land of democracy. That is what we got beat up for. It was as simple as that."

Bill Traylor

It Jes' Happened: When Bill Traylor Started to Draw. By Don Tate. Illustrated by R. Gregory Christie. Lee & Low Books, 2012. 32 p. Ages 5–10.

Bill Traylor started drawing for the first time at the age of eighty-five years old. If people asked him why, "he might have said, 'It jes' come to me.'" Bill was born a slave in Alabama. He worked hard but was able to enjoy some free time, swimming with friends. He stored these memories "deep inside himself." When the Civil War freed slaves, Bill and his family stayed on the farm as sharecroppers. When Bill was an old man, his wife had died and his children had scattered. He moved to the city and became homeless. "One day in early 1939 he picked up the stub of a pencil and a piece of discarded paper and began to pour out his memories in pictures." Several people admired his drawings. One person in particular, an artist named Charles Shannon, brought Bill art supplies; Charles also arranged for an exhibit of Bill's works. "Bill Traylor shared his memories with the world."

Sojourner Truth

Sojourner Truth's Step-Stomp Stride. By Andrea Davis Pinkney. Illustrated by Brian Pinkney. Jump at the Sun, 2009. 32 p. Ages 5–10.

Isabella, or Belle, was a slave who grew to almost six feet tall while she was still a young girl. When she was nine years old, Belle was sold and separated from her parents. She ran away and met up with a Quaker couple named Van Wagener, who helped her gain her freedom. Belle changed her name to Sojourner Truth. "She said the name Sojourner was just right for someone who was a traveler. And Truth—well, that was what Sojourner did best—she told it like it was." She spoke out against slavery and had her story told with the publication of *The Narrative of Sojourner Truth: A Northern Slave.* At one point, Sojourner stepped to the front of a church, stormed past men who had spoken against women's rights, and "*stomped* on the floorboards of ignorance." She told the gathering, "Ain't I a woman?" She argued that no man worked harder than her. And she walked out, "Big. Black. Beautiful. True."

Harriet Tubman

Moses: When Harriet Tubman Led Her People to Freedom. By Carole Boston Weatherford. Illustrated by Kadir Nelson. Jump at the Sun, 2006. 48 p. Ages 5–10.

Harriet set her mind to be free from her master and the plantation. She found comfort in her dialogues with God, who told her, "I SET THE NORTH STAR IN THE HEAVENS AND I MEAN FOR YOU TO BE FREE." Harriet traveled at night through swampland and forests. Men passed her but failed to see her. Harriet thanked God for "watching over me." She made her way to a farm she knew was a safe haven. The farmer helped Harriet get a little farther north. Whenever Harriet felt too weary to continue, the voice of God reminded her that "YOUR FAITH HAS WINGS." When Harriet arrived on free soil, she was encouraged to serve as a "conductor" on the Underground Railroad. "HARRIET, BE THE MOSES OF YOUR PEOPLE." The author's note informs us that Harriet "had gone south nineteen times and freed as many as three hundred slaves. She never lost a passenger." There are three sets of narrative indicated by the typeset: the narrator's perspective has normal type, Harriet's voice is written in italics, and God's voice appears all in caps.

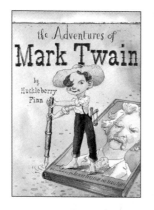

Mark Twain

The Adventures of Mark Twain by Huckleberry Finn. By Robert Burleigh. Illustrated by Barry Blitt. Atheneum, 2011. 48 p. Ages 8–12.

Mark Twain's literary creation Huck Finn has the unusual honor of narrating this biography. Huck warns us that this "ain't intending to be some windy bioografy." Huck gives a folksy look at the real aspects of Mark's life. We learn the inspiration behind Mark's pseudonym: "Folks'd let down a rope or chain to test the depth of the water. 'Mark Twain' they'd call out when the river was deep enough for the boat to pass." Huck also mentions that Mark wrote *The Adventures of Tom Sawyer*, "wherein I plays a very important part myself, if it don't seem like peacockin' to say so." Of course, he earned star billing in *The Adventures of Huckleberry Finn*. Mark Twain went on to become one of the biggest celebrities in the world.

Also highly recommended: *The Trouble Begins at 8: A Life of Mark Twain in the Wild, Wild West.* By Sid Fleischman. Greenwillow, 2008. 224 p. Ages 10–14. The title refers to humorist Mark Twain's first public speaking engagement: a poster read that the doors would open at seven and that "The Trouble to begin at 8 o'clock."

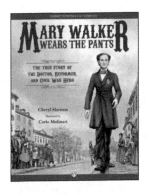

Mary Edwards Walker

Mary Walker Wears the Pants: The True Story of the Doctor, Reformer, and Civil War Hero. By Cheryl Harness. Illustrated by Carlo Molinari. Albert Whitman, 2013. 32 p. Ages 7–10.

Mary Walker fought convention by wearing pants and a suit coat. She campaigned for women's rights and went on to become one of the nation's first female physicians. During the Civil War, Mary tried to join the army as a surgeon but was refused several times. Finally, in 1863, she officially became "an assistant surgeon in the U.S. Army—a first for the military and a first for women." One day, Mary was captured by Confederate soldiers. They accused her of being a spy and sent her to a prison in Richmond, Virginia. Mary was eventually released in exchange for a Confederate surgeon. After the war was over, she received the Medal of Honor from President Andrew Johnson. "Countless courageous women had served their country, but none had *ever* had her valor so recognized." Still, Mary was often ridiculed for her clothing, even late in life, by people who were unaware of her accomplishments. Mary stuck to her convictions. "I wish it understood that I wear this style of dress from the highest, the purest and the noblest principle!"

Sarah Breedlove Walker

Vision of Beauty: The Story of Sarah Breedlove Walker. By Kathryn Lasky. Illustrated by Nneka Bennett. Candlewick, 2000. 48 p. Ages 8–12.

Sarah got married when she was fourteen and was widowed at the age of seventeen. She was worried about going bald due to years of poor nutrition and hard work. Sarah experimented with formulas that made her hair healthier. She went into business selling African American women's hair products. She used herself as the model in her ads, and the message of self-worth made an impact on African American women. Sarah married Charles Walker in 1905 and named her company the Mme. C. J. Walker Manufacturing Company.

Sarah felt the word "'*madame*' conveyed an image of status and dignity." Her business became a great success. One evening, she went to buy a movie ticket and was treated harshly by the white ticket taker because Sarah was black. Sarah had the last laugh when she built her own theater for African Americans. Sarah went on to become the richest African American woman in the country. She proved herself to be the equal of any male business owner. When Sarah died, her last words were, "I want to live to help my race."

George Washington

Washington at Valley Forge. By Russell Freedman. Holiday House, 2008. 100 p. Ages 10–14.

George Washington was reluctant to take command of the American Continental Army, a "makeshift army of volunteers with sketchy training and scarcely enough gunpowder to keep their muskets firing." His soldiers lost many battles before George changed his strategy to fight a defensive war. George selected Valley Forge as his winter camp to allow his troops to reorganize. They almost didn't make it. The thirteen-mile march took a whole week to travel. Some of his men were barefoot, leaving behind a trail of blood on the rough terrain. A large number of his soldiers were teenagers. Some were African Americans, some were American Indians, and about 450 women and children were also in or near the camp. At last, the army got into fighting shape. "The turning point came when the Continental Army survived the winter at Valley Forge and emerged tested and toughened as an effective fighting force."

Also highly recommended: *Revolutionary Friends: General George Washington and the Marquis de Lafayette.* By Selene Castrovilla. Illustrated by Drazen Kozjan. Calkins Creek, 2013. 40 p. Ages 7–12. This biography is sprinkled with French words to accent Lafayette's joy of being in the presence of Washington.

Noah Webster

Noah Webster & His Words. By Jeri Chase Ferris. Illustrated by Vincent X. Kirsch. Houghton Mifflin, 2012. 32 p. Ages 7–12.

Noah Webster was "full of CON-FI-DENCE [noun: belief that one is right]." He knew he didn't want to be a farmer like his father. When he was caught reading instead of doing his chores, "Noah was red-faced with EM-BAR-RASS-MENT [noun: shame; confusion]." He went on to become a teacher. Noah also wrote an American spelling book. Although it was a best seller, Noah didn't become wealthy; the printers got most of the profits. After several years of writing, Noah decided to write the first American "DIC-TION-AR-Y [noun: a book listing words in ABC order, telling what they mean and how to spell them]." He started it in 1807, studying and traveling to accomplish his dream. Noah finally finished his last entry: "ZY-GO-MAT-IC [adj.: related to the cheekbone]." He was "EC-STAT-IC [adj.: filled with pleasure; delighted; thrilled]!" The American Dictionary of the English Language was published in 1828, when Noah was seventy years old. Today, his dictionary remains "the second most ever popular book printed in English, after the Bible."

Ela Weissberger

The Cat with the Yellow Star: Coming of Age in Terezin. By Susan Goldman Rubin and Ela Weissberger. Holiday House, 2006. 40 p. Ages 9–14.

When Ela was eight years old, her father spoke out against Adolf Hitler. That night, he was taken away by police and was never seen again. Ela, her sister, and her mother left Sudetenland for Czechoslovakia. All Jews were ordered to wear yellow stars. In December 1941, eleven-year-old Ela and other family members were transported to Terezin, a concentration camp. She lived in a room with twenty-eight girls. There, the girls each received "about an ounce of margarine, maybe a spoon of some kind of marmalade, and a little piece of black bread." This had to last them for three or four days. To keep the girls' spirits up, one of the caretakers put on the opera show *Brundibár*. Ela was cast in the role of a cat. "When we were onstage, it was the only time we were allowed to remove our yellow stars." Years after she was liberated, Ela was invited onstage following a 2003 Los Angeles production of *Brundibár*, where she led the audience in a rendition of the victory march.

Phillis Wheatley

Phillis's Big Test. By Catherine Clinton. Illustrated by Sean Qualls. Houghton Mifflin, 2008. 32 p. Ages 5–10.

In 1773, Phillis became the first African American to have a book of poetry published. She had to first convince a committee of white males that she, a teenage slave girl, actually wrote the poems herself. Eleven years earlier, she had crossed the Atlantic Ocean on a slave ship from her homeland in Africa. She was bought by John Wheatley of Boston as a servant for his wife, Susanna. The Wheatleys were interested in educating Phillis, and she soon "spent more time on her studies than on serving her mistress." Phillis learned to read the Bible and poetry. This inspired her to write her own poems and recite them to the Wheatleys' friends. Phillis was not sure why she was transported to Boston from Africa, but she knew she wanted her voice to be heard. She wrote so that her books "would be there for her children and her children's children." Susanna gave Phillis this advice before she stood in front of her examiners: "Your talent will speak for itself." The epilogue informs us that Phillis did indeed pass her test, did publish her book, and was granted her freedom by the Wheatleys.

Simon Wiesenthal

The Anne Frank Case: Simon Wiesenthal's Search for the Truth. By Susan Goldman Rubin. Illustrated by Bill Farnsworth. Holiday House, 2009. 40 p. Ages 10–14.

Holocaust survivor and Nazi hunter Simon Wiesenthal set out to prove to doubters that Anne Frank's diary and the Holocaust actually happened. Simon searched for the unknown Gestapo soldier who had arrested Anne Frank as proof. Simon's own survival story in the Nazi concentration camps is miraculous. He was repeatedly lined up for execution, but circumstances halted several attempts. When the Allies arrived, Simon, who was nearly six feet tall, weighed only ninety-nine pounds. He provided valuable information about war criminals. "Helping the Americans gave him a purpose. 'Someone had to live on and tell what it was really like.'" In 1947, Simon established the Historical Document Center to bring Nazi criminals to trial and record their crimes. To find Anne Frank's officer, he started with her diary and looked for clues. This mission took Simon five years. The former Gestapo officer had been working the past years in a police headquarters just a short walk from Simon's office. Simon said, in memory of the Holocaust victims, "I didn't forget you."

Wild Boy of Aveyron

Wild Boy: The Real Life of the Savage of Aveyron. By Mary Losure. Candlewick, 2013. 169 p. Ages 10–14.

In 1798, a group of woodsmen captured a boy who had been living alone in the woods. The boy, who appeared to be around ten years old, was naked and could not speak. He escaped, but a year later was caught again. He escaped once again to the woods, and word spread throughout the land of this wild boy. The next time he was caught, he was sent first to an orphanage and then to the Institute for Deaf-Mutes. The Savage of Aveyron was given the name Victor. "It had a nice ring to it. A victor—a winner—is someone who triumphs over all obstacles."

Unfortunately, his teacher, Dr. Itard, considered the years spent with Victor a failure. "Sometimes he wondered whether it had been right, so long ago, to tear the boy from his old, happy life in the forest and bring him to live in Paris." When Victor was twenty-two years old, the Institute for Deaf-Mutes found him a new home. He was often recognized by locals as *le Sauvage*. Here, "he could do whatever he wanted, for the rest of his life."

Anna May Wong

Shining Star: The Anna May Wong Story.
By Paula Yoo. Illustrated by Lin Wang. Lee & Low Books, 2009. 32 p. Ages 6–12.

Anna May grew up in Los Angeles's China-town, working hard at her family's laun-dry. She often daydreamed about being an actress. She sometimes skipped school to watch filming at a nearby movie set. Anna May eventually got a part as an extra, earning seven and a half dollars each day. She appeared as an extra in several more movies, getting the attention of movie critics because of her "large, expressive eyes and ability to convey emotion with graceful hand movements." Anna May finally got a starring role working with the famous Lon Chaney. She was upset, however, when she saw that the "yellowface" makeup being applied to the white actors reinforced ste-reotypes of Chinese people. Anna May visited China for the first time to learn more about her culture and promised to "never play again in a film which shows the Chinese in an unsympathetic light." When she returned to Holly-wood, she played the first of many positive roles in the 1937 movie *Daughter of Shanghai*—"and for the first time in her life, she truly felt like a shining star."

Victoria Woodhull

A Woman for President: The Story of Victoria Woodhull. By Kathleen Krull.
Illustrated by Jane Dyer. Walker, 2004. 32 p. Ages 7–12.

Victoria traveled from town to town with her sister as fortune-tellers and faith healers. Along the way they met Cornelius Vanderbilt, the richest man in America. Victoria gave him financial advice and because of it, wound up becoming a millionaire herself. She used her wealth to help support women's rights. Once, Victoria and her sister entered a restaurant. They were told they couldn't be served since they were unaccompanied by a man. Victoria brought in her carriage driver and ordered soup for three. Women couldn't vote by law, but Victoria learned that there weren't any laws to prevent them from running for office. She declared her candidacy for president of the United States for the 1872 election. Many newspapers didn't take her seriously: "They called her women supporters as homely as 'nutmeg graters.'" After Victoria created the Equal Rights Party, the papers called the seven hundred delegates "wild men and women . . . strange-looking people." The party did nominate and support Victoria. "It was a wild moment in American history, and times would never be the same for women."

THE WRIGHT BROTHERS
How They Invented the Airplane

Russell Freedman
With Original Photographs by Wilbur and Orville Wright

Wilbur and Orville Wright

The Wright Brothers: How They Invented the Airplane. By Russell Freedman. Holiday House, 1991. 128 p. Ages 10–14.

Wilbur and his younger brother, Orville, were inseparable. Their interest in flight began when their father brought home a toy helicopter. The brothers also enjoyed tinkering with objects, an aptitude they claimed came from their mother because "their father had trouble driving a nail straight." They opened a printing shop and then a bicycle store. They also studied birds in flight and found the perfect site to work on their gliders—Kitty Hawk, North Carolina. After a series of failures, a dejected Wilbur exclaimed, "I made the prediction that man would sometime fly, but that it would not be in our lifetime." The brothers constantly made changes and built their own engine when they felt their glider was ready. Finally, Orville flew their machine, *The Flyer,* for twelve seconds. During a flying exhibition in France, one French pilot declared, "We are as children compared to the Wrights."

Also highly recommended: *To Fly: The Story of the Wright Brothers.* By Wendie Old. Illustrated by Robert Andrew Parker. Clarion, 2002. 48 p. 5–10. This picture book biography of the brothers' lives is formatted in page-length chapters.

Ed Young

The House Baba Built: An Artist's Childhood in China. By Ed Young and Libby Koponen. Illustrated by Ed Young. Little, Brown, 2011. 48 p. Ages 8–12.

With World War II looming, Ed Young's father, Baba, moved his wife and five children to the safest section of Shanghai. Baba made a proposal to the landowners: he would build a "big brick house on it, with courtyards, gardens, a swimming pool, and let the landowner have it all—after we had lived there for twenty years." The proposal was accepted and the large house was built. Young shares many childhood memories of the house Baba built, playing hide-

and-seek with cousins, roller-skating on the roof, and drawing. At one point, the children were forced to learn Japanese "but out of patriotism, everyone made a point of doing poorly in that class." Another time, Baba made an apartment to help two German refugees and their baby daughter, Jean. Young's sisters called the little girl Lu Mei Li, or Beautiful Sister. "And then, suddenly and unbelievably, the war was over. The first thing I said was, 'Now we can have meat again.'" The family celebrated "in the house Baba built."

Babe Didrikson Zaharias
Babe Didrikson Zaharias: The Making of a Champion. By Russell Freedman. Clarion, 1999. 192 p. Ages 10–14.

Even as a young child, Babe wanted "to be the best athlete that ever lived." She became accomplished in basketball, track and field, golf, tennis, baseball, diving, roller skating, and bowling. And as a second grader, she won a marble championship. When asked by a reporter if there wasn't anything she didn't play, Babe responded, "Yeah, dolls." As a young adult, Babe entered a national track and field competition as the sole member of her team. She won the meet by herself, prompting a reporter to write about, "the most amazing series of performances ever accomplished by any individual, male or female, in track and field history." Babe qualified for the 1932 Olympics and won two gold medals and a silver medal. One quote stated, "She's capable of winning everything but the Kentucky Derby." Her strong personality offended some, but made admirers of others. Babe entered a golf tournament and said, "Okay, Babe's here! Now, who's gonna finish second?" Babe's childhood dream came true when she was named the Top Female Athlete of the Half Century by the Associated Press.

Kenichi Zenimura
Barbed Wire Baseball. By Marissa Moss. Illustrated by Yuko Shimizu. Abrams, 2013. 42 p. Ages 5–10.

Zeni was small, barely five feet tall, but "when Zeni had a ball or bat in his hand, he felt like a giant. And soon he played like one." Zeni played exhibition games in Japan with the New York Yankees. When Pearl Harbor was attacked in 1941, Zeni and other Japanese Americans were sent to internment camps. He decided to make a baseball field in the dry, brown and gray desert earth. Dozens of people helped out, chopping plants and digging up rocks in the heat. Zeni got permission from the camp commander to use the base's bulldozer to level the field. Zeni next diverted an irrigation pipe to cut down on dust, and to grow grass for the infield and castor beans to mark the edge of the outfield. Flour was used to mark baselines; rice sacks were sewn together to make bases; "several women sewed uniforms out of potato sacks." Once the games began, Zeni felt free again. The author's notes mention that after the war, Zeni was inducted into the Shrine of the Eternals, the national equivalent to the National Baseball Hall of Fame.

Zishe

Zishe the Strongman. By Robert Rubinstein. Illustrated by Woody Miller. Kar-Ben, 2010. 32 p. Ages 4–9.

Zishe was the son of a blacksmith in Poland. At the age of three, he imitated his father and swung a nine-pound hammer through the air and brought it down on an anvil. As he grew, the other children in his village would bring him metal bars to bend to test his strength. Zishe was also a gentle child who loved animals and playing his cello. Zishe left his village and performed in a traveling circus all over Europe. For one feat, "an elephant would walk over a bridge built across his chest." Zishe made sure to visit the Jewish communities wherever he traveled. The children would call him Samson. He did the same thing in America. "Zishe would take time to visit his fellow Jews. Often he would play his cello for children at local hospitals. His heart was as great as his strength." Zishe performed a unique act in New York City: he pulled a wagonload of ten men for a half mile down Fifth Avenue with his teeth. "It was the crowning achievement for the Iron King!"

CHAPTER **2**

Collective Biographies

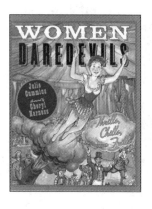

Women Daredevils: Thrills, Chills, and Frills

By *Julie Cummins*. Illustrated by Cheryl Harness. Dutton, 2008. 48 p. Ages 8–12.

Long before modern extreme sports appeared on television, several daredevils risked their lives in a variety of ways to entertain audiences in the late 1800s and early 1900s. Fourteen female daredevils "hiked up their skirts and scoffed at public disapproval with their incredible acts that were enough to scare the pants off most men." Among them were Rosa "Zazel" Richter, a circus human cannonball; Isabelle Butler, who performed a car stunt called "The Dip of Death"; the La Rague Sisters, who performed double-car stunts; Georgia "Tiny" Broadwick, the first female to parachute from a plane; Mabel Stark, a tiger trainer-tamer; Sonora Webster Carver, who rode high-diving horses; and Gertrude Breton, a daredevil bicyclist. When talking about danger and risks, Breton gave perhaps the best quote from the book: "I have had some accidents myself. One was in Kansas City last year. I

Figure 2.1. From **Women Daredevils: Thrills, Chills, and Frills**
by Julie Cummins, illustrated by Cheryl Harness.

would not have been hurt but for the fact that a policeman who tried to catch me inadvertently struck my head with his club."

We Were There, Too! Young People in History
By Phillip Hoose. Farrar, Straus and Giroux, 2001. 264 p. Ages 10–14.

Young people played important roles throughout U.S. history. Diego Bermúdez was a twelve-year-old who sailed with Columbus on the Santa Maria in 1492. Diego served as a "singing clock" by singing out a prayer to let the crew know how much time remained on their shifts. The Bermuda Islands were named after Diego's brother Juan. When Columbus made his fourth voyage to the new world, fifty-six of the ninety-nine crew members were eighteen years or younger. Biographer Hoose follows up with a look at the young population of the Taino people, the indigenous population Columbus encountered. "Anthropologists conclude that at least half of all Tainos were fifteen or younger." This collection of short biographies showcases well-known young people such as Pocahontas, Frederic Douglass, Sacagawea, and Bill Gates, as well as lesser-known figures from history. Among these are Anyokah, the six-year-old daughter of Sequoyah, who helped her father develop the Cherokee syllabic alphabet, and Kory Johnson, a young girl from a poor neighborhood who helped create Children for a Safe Environment to keep communities clean from pollutants.

The Dark Game: True Spy Stories
By Paul B. Janeczko. Candlewick, 2010. 248p. Ages 10–14.

Biographer Janeczko recognizes the importance of George Washington's spy system when he states that in addition to being named the "father of our country," Washington could also be called "the father of American espionage." A British major stated that "Washington did not really outfit the British, he simply outspied us." During the Civil War, Washington socialite Rose O'Neale Greenhow was a successful spymaster whose information may have helped the South defeat the North in the important Battle of Bull Run. Even after she was captured by Pinkerton agents and sent to prison, she smuggled out code via the colors of yarn in her tapestries. There are some humorous moments in the book. During World War II, Virginia Hall spied on the Germans for the Allies. She had a wooden leg she named Cuthbert. While fleeing the Gestapo over a mountainous terrain, she sent a message that Cuthbert was giving her trouble. A radio operator unfamiliar with this pet name replied, "If Cuthbert is giving you trouble, have him eliminated."

Lives of Extraordinary Women: Rulers, Rebels (and What the Neighbors Thought)
By Kathleen Krull. Illustrated by Kathryn Hewitt. Harcourt, 2000. 95 p. Ages 9–14.

Twenty women who held political positions throughout history are profiled, including "the good, the bad, and some who were both." Gertrude Bell, a British government official who loved the Middle East, "never flinched at the sheep's eyes served to her as an honored guest." Eva Peron, first lady of Argentina, had the habit of nibbling on her jewelry. She once "ended up with green lips when her necklace turned out to be made of painted noodles." Biographer Krull acknowledges that these profiles "inspire awe at the power of women."

Also highly recommended: *Lives of the Musicians: Good Times, Bad Times (and What the Neighbors Thought).* By Kathleen Krull. Illustrated by Kathryn Hewitt. Harcourt, 1993. 95 p. Ages 10–14. This is the first in the Lives Of series. The other titles are *Lives of the Writers: Comedies, Tragedies (and What the Neighbors Thought)* (1994), *Lives of the Artists: Masterpieces, Messes (and What the Neighbors Thought)* (1995), *Lives of the Athletes: Thrills, Spills (and What the Neighbors Thought)* (1997), *Lives of the Presidents: Fame, Shame (and What the Neighbors Thought)* (1998), *Lives of the Pirates: Swashbucklers, Scoundrels (Neighbors Beware!)* (2010), and *Lives of the Scientists: Experiments, Explosions (and What the Neighbors Thought)* (2013).

The Beatles Were Fab (and They Were Funny)

By Kathleen Krull and Paul Brewer. Illustrated by Stacy Innerst. Harcourt, 2013. 32p. Ages 5–10.

Beatlemania grabbed the world's attention in the 1960s. The four Beatles were not only musically talented, but they also had wonderful senses of humor. Their producer was initially very critical of their music. He told them to let him know if there was anything they didn't like. George Harrison replied, "Well, for a start, I don't like your tie." When the band played a concert that the royal family attended, John Lennon invited everyone to clap along. He then looked up at the box seats and said, "And the rest of you, if you just rattle your jewelry." Paul McCartney told reporters that his favorite sport was sleeping. A reporter asked Ringo "How did you find America?" Ringo Starr replied, "We went to Greenland and made a left turn." The four lads started playing small clubs in Liverpool, England, and they went on to play huge concerts in baseball stadiums. They eventually stopped performing live and "retreated to the recording studio, where they could hear the music again and continue to make each other laugh."

Let It Shine: Stories of Black Women Freedom Fighters
By Andrea Davis Pinkney. Harcourt, 2000. 107 p. Ages 10–14.

Biographer Pinkney weaves together the stories of ten women whose lives are intertwined as "one incredible story—a story of the challenges and triumphs of civil rights that spanned American history from the eighteenth century to the present day." Biddy Mason was forced to walk from the East Coast to Utah in 1848 when her master moved everything he owned, including Biddy. A few years later, she had to walk to California. Biddy managed to win her freedom through clever action and was even able to buy a house (it cost $250 at the time). She became one of the wealthiest African American women in Los Angeles. The other women profiled in this collection are Ella Josephine Baker, Mary McLeod Bethune, Shirley Chisholm, Fannie Lou Hamer, Dorothy Irene Height, Rosa Parks, Sojourner Truth, Harriet Tubman, and Ida B. Wells-Barnett.

Also highly recommended: *Hand in Hand: Ten Black Men Who Changed America.* By Andrea Davis Pinkney. Jump at the Sun, 2012. 243 p. Ages 10–14. Pinkney profiles Benjamin Banneker, Frederick Douglass, Booker T. Washington, W. E. B. DuBois, A. Philip Randolph, Thurgood Marshall, Jackie Robinson, Malcolm X, Martin Luther King Jr., and Barack H. Obama Jr.

Almost Astronauts: 13 Women Who Dared to Dream
By Tanya Lee Stone. Candlewick, 2009. 133 p. Ages 10–14.

In the early 1960s, during NASA's Mercury program to put men into space, thirteen female pilots were tested to see if they had "the right stuff" to become astronauts. They passed the extreme testing with flying colors, sometimes surpassing the males. Unfortunately, they were met with resistance solely because of their gender: "It didn't matter that the women were qualified . . . sending a woman to do a man's job would not project the image of international strength that (President) Kennedy desired." When the women fought back, the research was shut down due to negative influences of not only military administrators, but also the male astronauts, one influential female pilot who was rejected for the testing, and finally Lyndon Baines Johnson, who made this eye-opening quote: "If we let you or other women into the space program, we'd have to let blacks in. We'd have to let Mexican Americans in, and Chinese Americans. We'd have to let every minority in, and we just can't do that." The opening chapter is titled "T Minus Thirty-Eight Years." It is July 1999, and the women featured in the book are witnesses to the launching of the first female space shuttle commander.

Girls Think of Everything: Stories of Ingenious Inventions by Women
By Catherine Thimmesh. Houghton Mifflin, 2000. 58 p. Ages 10–14.

Women have invented several products over the years, "but their accomplishments have often been downplayed, skimmed over, or ignored altogether."

This book goes into detail for twelve inventions, including windshield wipers, Kevlar, Scotchgard, the space bumper that protects spacecrafts from debris, and even the paper bag. One chapter features Bette Nesmith Graham, an executive secretary who invented Liquid Paper, also known as "white-out." She made batches of what she first called "Mistake Out" in her kitchen and garage. After an article about her product appeared in a trade publication, orders flooded in and she became a multimillionaire. (Her son, Michael, later became a member of the television music show group *The Monkees* and used part of his inheritance to create a production company.) The final two stories feature young inventors. Becky Schroeder invented the Glo-sheet when she was ten years old, "the youngest female ever to receive a U.S. patent." Eleven-year-old Alexia Abernathy created the no-spill pet feeding bowl that was later sold in stores such as Wal-Mart and Target.

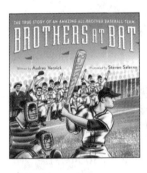

Brothers at Bat: The True Story of an Amazing All-Brother Baseball Team
By Audrey Vernick. Illustrated by Steven Salerno. Houghton Mifflin, 2012. 40 p. Ages 5–10.

The Accera family consisted of four girls and twelve boys. "Their high school baseball team had an Accera on it twenty-two years in a row!" In 1938, the oldest brothers organized a semipro team that their father coached. Anthony was nicknamed "Poser" because of the way he stood at the plate, Jimmy had a great knuckleball and was considered to be the best player, and Alfred was a solid catcher even though he lost the use of one eye in a baseball accident. World War II took many of the brothers into service, but when the war was over, they once again played ball. They won the Long Branch City Twilight Baseball League championship four times in six years. In 1997, a special honor was held for the Accera family at the National Baseball Hall of Fame. On the way home from the ceremony, their bus broke down. While they waited by the side of the road, everyone played baseball. "That ball soared from grandfather to granddaughter, from father to son. From brother to brother."

Bad Girls: Sirens, Jezebels, Murderesses, Thieves & Other Female Villains
By Jane Yolen and Heidi E. Y. Stemple. Charlesbridge, 2013. 164 p. Ages 12–14.

The twenty-six females profiled in this collection are called "the baddest of the bad, as well as those who may have just been misunderstood." Elizabeth

Bathory is arguably the most gruesome character in the collection, as she bathed in the blood of perhaps five hundred victims. One interesting fairly unknown figure is Pearl Hart, a Canadian who ran off to America to become a stagecoach robber. Once, after Pearl and her partners robbed three passengers, "Pearl felt bad so she returned a dollar to each, 'for grub and lodging.'" In between each profile is a one-page comic-formatted exchange between biographers Yolen and Stemple, who express their opinions about each character with a touch of levity. The collection ends with a quote from Jessica Rabbit from the movie *Who Framed Roger Rabbit*: "I'm not bad. I'm just drawn that way."

Also highly recommended: *Sea Queens: Women Pirates around the World.* By Jane Yolen. Illustrated by Christine Joy Pratt. Charlesbridge, 2008. 104 p. Ages 10–14. Thirteen female pirates are profiled, from Artemisia of Persia (500–480 BC) to Madame Ching of China in the early nineteenth century.

CHAPTER 3

Finding the Treasure Trove

AN INTERVIEW WITH AUTHOR ROBERT BURLEIGH

Robert Burleigh is the author of more than forty children's books, including many creative biographies for young people. Some of his more inventive biographies include *The Adventures of Mark Twain by Huckleberry Finn* (p. 93) and *Into the Woods: John James Audubon Lives His Dream* (p. 7). Other biographies by Robert included in this guide are *Black Whiteness: Admiral Byrd Alone in the Antarctic* (p. 17), *Look Up! Henrietta Leavitt, Pioneering Woman Astronomer* (p. 52), *Flight: The Journey of Charles Lindbergh* (p. 55), and *Tiger of the Snows: Tenzing Norgay: The Boy Whose Dream Was Everest* (p. 66). A complete list of Robert's books can be found at his website, www.robert burleigh.com.

Why do you write biographies for young people?

ROBERT BURLEIGH: I have always had an interest in how people, famous and otherwise, make their way through life. I think everyone's life is a treasure trove, but of course due to the way the world operates, I can't expect to publish (as easily) the life story of my next-door neighbor. I like to read about a person's life and pick out a dramatic moment and go from there.

How do you choose the person you are going to research and write about?

RB: Pretty much by chance. I read a good deal, and keep my ears open too.

As you know, some people are in and some not at any given time, but in general, I just choose and see what happens. Since I read more in Americana, most of my subjects have come from American history, but not all. Also, I do sometimes try the subject out on an editor first, to see how he or she responds to the idea.

Do have any favorites of the people you've written about?

RB: When I visit schools, I'm always asked: "What's your favorite book—of those you've written." My usual answer is "The one I'm working on right now," which is more or less true. But perhaps if I had to choose, I'd pick my biography of Audubon because I used it to argue for art's significant place in the world; or maybe the Twain book you mentioned, because I thought the idea of using Huck Finn as "author" was a fun idea.

How do you choose which style you are going to tell a person's story?

RB: I let the character, and even more, the angle I feel like taking dictate that. Recently I've started to think in terms of first-person presentations. I think this allows me to give a more personal picture of the subject.

Have you seen biographies for young people change over the years? Are there any trends that you've observed?

RB: If any, I think there is an opening up of bio subjects as well as more leeway regarding the tone one can take toward the subject. In other words, the author doesn't have to approach every "great or famous" person with a heavily reverent attitude. You can treat many subjects more lightly or more tangentially. You don't have to tell the whole life of the person, maybe just a funny or significant part of the life.

CHAPTER **4**

"Every Book Has a Different Answer"

AN INTERVIEW WITH AUTHOR KATHLEEN KRULL

Kathleen Krull has written over two dozen biography books for young people, including her unique, popular Lives Of series that focuses on fun aspects of famous people's lives. Kathleen is the recipient of the 2011 Children's Book Guild of Washington, DC, Nonfiction Award Winner for Body of Work. In addition to the Lives Of books, Kathleen's other biographies profiled in this guide are *Albert Einstein* (p. 31), *The Beatles Were Fab (and They Were Funny)* (p. 106), *The Boy on Fairfield Street: How Ted Geisel Grew Up to Become Dr. Seuss* (p. 83), *The Boy Who Invented TV: The Story of Philo Farnsworth* (p. 33), *Harvesting Hope: The Story of Cesar Chavez* (p. 19), *Houdini: World's Greatest Mystery Man and Escape King* (p. 43), *Louisa May's Battle: How the Civil War Led to Little Women* (p. 2), and *Wilma Unlimited: How Wilma Rudolph Became the World's Fastest Woman* (p. 77). For more about Kathleen Krull, visit her website, www.kathleenkrull.com.

Why do you write biographies for young people?

KATHLEEN KRULL: Money. Just kidding. But with a goal of being a self-supporting writer, I was floundering before my book *Lives of the Musicians* was published. I wrote short stories to send to the *New Yorker* (getting occasional scribbles back), two semiautobiographical chapter books about a girl named Alex Fitzgerald, several picture books and collections of music, and a book for adults about how to write a book, all while growing more impoverished by the day. Years in the making, *Lives of the Musicians* was pitched as a joint endeavor with the artist, the amazing Kathryn Hewitt. I minored in music in college—it's one of my passions—and when I looked at the biographies in the 1980s, musical and otherwise, I wanted to do something fresher and more relevant to contemporary kids. When the book finally came out in 1993 and won several awards, I felt like I had found a niche with a lifetime of compelling avenues to explore.

How do you choose who you are going to research and write about?

KK: I look for people I admire, especially who are neglected and deserve to be better known; subjects where competition is either nil or not that interesting. Sometimes editors and others give me ideas that strike a spark. But mainly, research for the ongoing Lives Of series has led me to other books. I'm always encountering people I want to learn more about. A good example: while researching Ulysses S. Grant for *Lives of the Presidents,* I ran into Victoria Woodhull, the first woman to run for president (against him), which inspired my biography of her.

Do you have any favorites of all the people you've written about?

KK: With the exception of the criminals in *Lives of the Pirates,* I love just about all of them—personal passion is one of my criteria for picking a person. But certain ones stand out:

- Beethoven: His was the sample chapter that we used to sell Lives of the Musicians. The material is so very spicy, and I love to talk about him, though I remain discouraged when kids think I'm talking about the dog;

- Victoria Woodhull: She was a pet project and a challenge, because no one had heard of her. Her life story isn't all that child friendly, and she's still ahead of her time;

- Wilma Rudolph and Cesar Chavez: Because I still choke up when reading these two books aloud;

- Dr. Seuss: One of my personal heroes and just about the only person I've written about whom I got to meet; and

- The Beatles: My husband, Paul Brewer, and I are total Beatlemaniacs. Last year we made a Beatle pilgrimage to Liverpool, London, and Hamburg.

How do you choose which style you are going to tell a particular person's story?

KK: No easy answer here. Maybe it's that every book has a different answer. I start by reading as widely as possible about the person, whatever I can get my hands on, but especially what the best scholars have written; not taking notes yet, just trying to tease out the best story to tell. This is one of the delicious parts of the process. At some point a sentence (or maybe two) will dance into my mind, something that tickles me, and I'll rush to write it down. That sentence probably won't make it into the final manuscript, but it jump-starts me into a way of thinking and writing, and I go on from there into a series of endless choices. That's the idea, anyway.

Have you seen biographies for young people in the industry change over the years? Are there any trends you've noticed?

KK: All I can say is—Doreen Rappaport, Deborah Hopkinson, Barbara Kerley, Jonah Winter, Jeanette Winter, Tanya Lee Stone, Jim Murphy, Tonya Bolden, Robert Burleigh, Don Brown, Pam Munoz Ryan, Andrea Davis Pinkney, Deborah Heiligman, Robert Byrd, Shana Corey, Kadir Nelson, Meghan McCarthy, Candace Fleming, and a slew of others—I think we're in a golden age of biographies for kids. Besides being more plentiful and much more child friendly, many are quirky or whimsical, and many are using original research normally done by writers for adults. I would argue that the choices I make qualify to make the results original, but I am not an academic. I see my role as taking the valuable work of the best scholars and distilling it into a form that I hope will make children love—or at least, like—history.

CHAPTER 5

"Not Household Names, but Should Be"

AN INTERVIEW WITH PUBLISHER JASON LOW

Jason Low is the current publisher of Lee & Low Books, founded in 1991 by Philip Lee and Tom Low, Jason's father. The company's stated mission is to "meet the need for stories that *all* children can identify with and enjoy." In addition to biographies, Lee & Low has published over 650 picture books, board books, bilingual books, children's and young novels, and graphic novels. There are over twenty Lee & Low biographies covering all aspects of diversity featured in this guide, including *Catching the Moon: The Story of a Young Girl's Baseball Dream* by Crystal Hubbard (p. 85), *Etched in Clay: The Life of Dave, Enslaved Potter and Poet* by Andrea Cheng (p. 27), *Passage to Freedom: The Sugihara Story* by Ken Mochizuki (p. 86), *Quiet Hero: The Ira Hayes Story* by S. D. Nelson (p. 40), *Seeds of Change: Planting a Path to Peace* by Jen Cullerton Johnson (p. 58), *Seven Miles to Freedom: The Robert Smalls Story* by Janet Halfmann (p. 84), and *Silent Star: The Story of Deaf Major Leaguer William Hoy* by Bill Wise (p. 43). Their website is www.leeandlow.com.

What factors go into deciding which biographies Lee & Low publishes?

JASON LOW: Since our mission focuses on diversity, our biographies tend to be about people of color. This is an important distinction because many of the people we have published books about are not household names, but should be. Peg Leg Bates, Duke Kahanamoku, Sammy Lee, John Lewis, Wangari Maathai, Robert Smalls, Toni Stone, and Anna May Wong are several individuals who have all defied the odds in their own ways and through their courage and unbending will have helped bring us closer to a world that is more balanced and equal.

What trends have you noticed in biographies for young people over the years?

JL: I see a lot of books being published about household names such as Jackie Robinson, Rosa Parks, and Martin Luther King Jr. While their stories are important, they are not the only ones that young people should know. It is vital to publish books that go beyond the few famous names to show children that acts of bravery are performed every day by ordinary people like them. This is the stuff that makes great biographies—and approachable ones too.

SUBJECT INDEX

INDEX